JAM JAM JAM

with
JOE SATRIANI

www.jamtrax.com

CONTENTS

ON THE CD

The CD is split into two sections; section 1 (tracks 1-8) is the backing tracks minus lead guitar and vocals, while section 2 (tracks 9-16) is the backing tracks with all guitar parts added, so in addition to the written tab you can hear the rhythm, fills, and solos as they should be played!

Music arranged by Jamie Humphries and produced by Steve Finch
Assistant Engineer, James Walker
Executive production, Steve Finch and Kim Waller
Recorded at the TOTAL ACCURACY SOUNDHOUSE, Romford, England

Guitars, Jamie Humphries
Bass and Bass programming, Mick Ash
Drums, Pete Riley
Keyboards, Alison Pearse
Drum programming, Steve Finch
Jamie Humphries uses Ernie Ball/Musicman guitars and Cornford amps
Road Rock Studios use Line 6 products

Music transcribed by Jamie Humphries
Cover Design by Kim Waller
Music engraved by Cambridge Notation

www.jamtrax.com

INTRODUCTION

The TOTAL ACCURACY *JAM with...* series is a powerful learning tool that will help you extend your stockpile of licks and fills and develop your improvisational skills. The combination of musical notation and guitar tablature in the book, together with backing tracks on the CD, give you the opportunity to learn each track note-for-note and then jam with a professional session band. The track listing reflects some of Joe Satriani's most popular recordings, providing something for guitarists to have fun with and improvise with, as well as something to aspire to.

The first eight tracks on the CD are full length backing tracks recorded minus lead guitar. The remaining tracks feature the backing tracks with the lead guitar parts added. Although many of you will have all the original tracks in your own collections, we have provided them in the package for your reference. The *JAM with...* series allows you to accurately recreate the original, or to use the transcriptions in this book in conjunction with the backing tracks as a basis for your own improvisation. For your benefit we have put definite endings on the backing tracks, rather than fading them out as is the case on some of the original recordings. The accompanying transcriptions correspond to our versions. Remember, experimenting with your own ideas is equally important for developing your own style; most important of all, however, is that you enjoy *JAM with Joe Satriani* and HAVE FUN!

JOE SATRIANI

Joe Satriani is one of the most well respected and successful instrumental guitarists in rock history. In a career spanning almost 20 years he has won countless awards for his compositions and his technical prowess on the guitar.

Born in Long Island, New York, in 1952, Joe started playing guitar the day that Jimi Hendrix died. Joe actually started out playing drums, but had a good understanding of music theory, and had also begun training his ears to recognise chords and scales. Joe began a rigorous practice schedule, as well as playing in high school bands performing music by Hendrix, Led Zeppelin, and Black Sabbath. At one point Joe also had the opportunity to study at Berklee, but found the environment too noisy and unorganised for him to work in.

Joe began teaching guitar at about the age of 15. One of his early students was Steve Vai. Steve could not play a note when he first went to Joe for his lessons; he turned up with an old guitar and a pack of strings that needed to be fitted! Many similarities have been drawn between Satch and Vai, and it's not surprising, as Joe was Vai's main influence at that time. Joe continued his work as a guitar teacher when he relocated to San Francisco. He taught a number of other well-respected and successful guitarists including Kirk Hammett of Metallica, Larry La Londe of Primus, Jeff Tyson of T Ride, and Alex Skolnick of Testament.

Joe was also working in an originals rock band called The Squares, but he was becoming frustrated because the band would never release anything by themselves, and instead were waiting to be signed by a major label. Joe realised that there were a lot of other bands doing the same kind of thing—releasing material themselves—and doing it better than The Squares. Joe realised things had to change, and set about changing them when The Squares took a three-week–long Christmas break in 1983.

Joe called in a favour at a local studio, and set about recording his *Joe Satriani* EP. The EP featured Joe's own instrumental compositions performed totally on the guitar. Joe tuned down the low string to achieve a bass guitar sound, and hit the guitar pickups with Allen keys to make drum-like noises. The EP consisted of five tracks. He set up his own publishing company as well called Strange Beautiful Music, and a small record label, named after his wife, called Rubina.

Joe continued to record four-track demos for an album, but was forced to shelve the project due to not being able to finance it. Joe then received a credit card and chequebook, with roughly a $5,000 limit, that enabled him to record the project. The album was titled *Not of This Earth*. Joe sent the album to ex-pupil and long time friend Steve Vai. Steve sent the album to his label, and the rest is history. The album included a set of awesome instrumentals including "Hordes Of Locusts," "The Snake," and the haunting ballad "Rubina."

Joe was yet to break the scene in a big way, although the album gained the attention of guitar magazines. But Joe was not aware of the impact that his next album would have on not just the guitar community, but the entire music industry. Joe went into the studio with the idea of creating an album that focused purely on the guitar, and was not concerned with what was natural or unnatural. He released *Surfing with the Alien* in 1988, and the album made the entire industry take instrumental rock seriously. At this time many of the rock guitar albums available concentrated on playing over-the-top runs and licks, with no real concern for a tune. But Joe managed to fuse catchy melodies with incredible technique. The album included the awesome title cut "Surfing with the Alien," the soulful ballad "Always with Me, Always with You," and the classic hyper blues, "Satch Boogie". The album took the Billboard chart by storm, and tracks were being requested frequently on the radio. Joe's dream had come true, with him finally hanging up his guitar teacher's cap and becoming a worldwide "Guitar God" alongside his hero Jimi Hendrix. Joe also put together his legendary power trio for the tour, with Stu Hamm on bass and Jonathan Mover on drums.

The success of *Surfing* added pressure when it came to Joe's next studio release. But he did not crumble, and hit back with *Flying in a Blue Dream*. This album had all the classic Satch trademarks, but also had a new twist, with Joe singing lead vocals on some of the tracks, including "Big Bad Moon" and "I Believe." The album also included possibly one of Joe's most incredible performances to date in the form of the title track, "Flying in a Blue Dream." This track included a classic haunting Lydian melody, plus Joe's seamless, fluid, legato lines. Once again the album was a huge success and won more awards and critical acclaim.

Joe wanted to change his sound for his next project and give it a more live feel as opposed to the techno overdub sound on some of his previous releases. Joe hooked up with legendary producer Andy Johns to record *The Extremist*. He also recruited Matt and Gregg Bissonette on bass and drums, respectively. The album included such tracks as "The Extremist," the sinister sounding "War," "Summer Song," and the soulful ballad "Crying." Most of the album was written on the *Flying in a Blue Dream* tour and, as with the previous albums, was a huge success.

After *The Extremist* tour, Joe's record company wanted to release a live album. Joe began sifting through tapes of live recordings and sessions that had never made it onto finished albums. Joe finally released *Time Machine*, a double album that included live material plus previously unreleased tracks and his four-track EP, *Joe Satriani*.

Joe's next album surprised fans and critics again when he released *Joe Satriani* in 1995. Again, Joe stuck with the raw, live sound of *The Extremist*, but captured a much looser feel. He also recruited many top class musicians including Nathan East on bass, Andy Fairweather Low on rhythm guitar, and Manu Katche on drums. This album included such tracks as "Slow Down Blues," "Killer Bee Bop", and "Cool #9," with its shrieking whammy pedal lines.

During the *Flying in a Blue Dream* tour, guitarist Eric Johnson joined Satch. Both decided that they wanted to work together again, but busy schedules did not allow it to happen. Satch had the idea of putting together a tour purely for the guitar. The result was the *G3* tour, consisting of three guitar heavy weights: Joe Satriani, Steve Vai, and Eric Johnson. Each guitarist would play a set, and then all three would join the stage for a jam. Johnson left the tour after the release of the *G3* album and video, but the *G3* legacy did not end there, with Satch inviting other guitarist's such as Robert Fripp, Kenny Wayne Shepherd, and Michael Schenker to join the tour.

Satch has more recently returned to the sound of *Surfing* with the release of *The Crystal Planet* and *Engines of Creation*, all of which fuse guitar with techno dance loops.

Joe Satriani is without a doubt one of the world's greatest rock guitarists. Not only has he recorded some of the most amazing solo guitar albums, but he has also worked as a hired sideman for the likes of Mick Jagger, Alice Cooper, and the spoof metal band Spinal Tap. Now, at the beginning of a new millennium, Satch is still the undisputed king of instrumental rock guitar.

PERFORMANCE NOTES

SURFING WITH THE ALIEN

This classic track clocks in at a rapid 171 bpm, and kicks off with a fast surf guitar–style riff. The main melodic theme uses notes from G minor pentatonic (G, B♭, C, D, F, G), and G Dorian (G, A, B♭, C, D, E, F, G), and should be performed with a wah pedal. The melody is embellished with quarter tone bends and whammy bar vibrato, plus the occasional pinched harmonic. The tune kicks up a gear at bar 25, with the melody using notes based around E minor pentatonic (E, G, A, B, D, E), C Mixolydian (C, D, E, F, G, A, B♭, C), plus some country-flavoured lines based around G major. This section also includes some of Joe's signature screaming harmonics and whammy dive bombs. This section repeats, with the melody lines being performed up at the 12th position.

The solo kicks in at bar 41, with Joe performing a rapid-fire tapping section. The tapped notes are produced by striking the string with the edge of the pick. This section uses notes from the C♯ Phrygian dominant scale (C♯, D, E♯, F♯, G♯, A, B, C♯). This section concludes with some fluid legato phrasing. The section continues and modulates through various different keys, all of which retain the Spanish Phrygian tonality. Bar 57 contains a pretty complex section that fuses both legato and picked ideas, plus some wide stretches.

The solo section concludes with a screaming harmonic at bar 63 that leads into a country-flavoured section based around G major pentatonic (G, A, B, D, E, G). The main melody is then reintroduced at bar 69.

The outro solo is introduced at bar 104 and includes a fast figure that outlines the G7 and C7 arpeggios and uses fast left hand slurs. This is followed by a short figure based around G Dorian, with each note being embellished with a whammy bar slur.

The song concludes with more G minor pentatonic phrasing plus the whammy melody and finally some rhythmic double-stops. This track was probably recorded with an Ibanez guitar and a Rockman preamp.

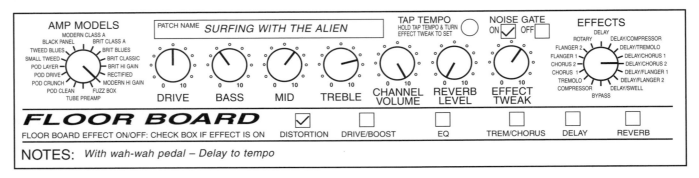

FLYING IN A BLUE DREAM

The title track from the album of the same name features possibly one of Joe's most memorable melodies and some seamless legato lines. The song kicks off with some feedback pitches, produced by changing the position of the guitar in front of the amplifier. The rhythm guitar doubles the keyboard part with a clean chord arpeggio figure, the guitar using open F tuning. The main melody is introduced at bar 19 and uses the C Lydian mode (C, D, E, F♯, G, A, B, C). The phrasing is very laid back and, in places, behind the beat. Joe uses more left hand slides and plenty of vibrato. At bar 27, Joe modulates to A♭ Lydian (A♭, B♭, C, D, E♭, F, G, A♭) before returning to C Lydian at bar 31. At bar 35 he includes notes from the G Lydian mode, (G, A, B, C♯, D, E, F♯, G) and, at bar 37, F Lydian (F, G, A, B, C, D, E, F). These modulations to other Lydian keys happen throughout the piece.

Bar 47 introduces the main solo and includes a long fluid legato pattern based around C Lydian. The run includes lots of position shifts, plus some two handed tapping. Bar 58 includes a whammy bar slurred section, based around A♭ Lydian. Bar 77 concludes the Lydian section of the solo with more legato phrasing. The final section of the solo starts at bar 79, and uses notes from G Dorian (G, A, B♭, C, D, E, F, G), and C Mixolydian (C, D, E, F, G, A, B♭, C), both diatonic modes to F major. This section includes some blues based lines and double-stop ideas. The solo concludes at bar 92 with another long legato line.

Bar 95 reintroduces the main melodic theme that continues to the end of the song, and includes some screaming harmonic whammy dives and more feedback notes. This song was probably recorded with an Ibanez guitar, possibly through a Rockman preamp.

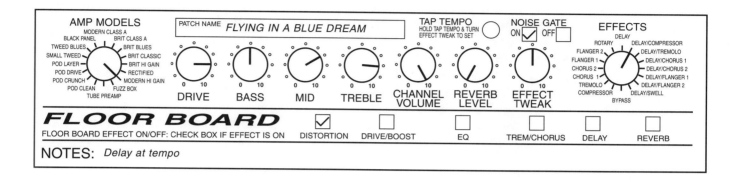

SUMMER SONG

This classic track can also be found on the *Extremist* album, and drives along at 160 bpm. The riff is an A Mixolydian progression based around the chords of A5 and Gmajor7/A, played against a driving A root note. At bar 5 a harmonic melody is introduced. The main melody is based around the A major pentatonic scale (A, B, C♯, E, F♯, A), A Mixolydian (A, B, C♯, D, E, F♯, G, A), and the modes diatonic to D major. The main melody is repeated in a different octave, a common part of Joe's compositions.

The chorus kicks in at bar 49, and uses both A Mixolydian and A minor pentatonic (A, C, D, E, G, A). The chorus includes bluesy bends and phrases, plus lines that compliment the progression. The solo section enters at bar 71 and uses notes from G minor pentatonic (G, B♭, C, D, F, G), and G Dorian (G, A, B, C, D, E, F♯, G). Bar 79 includes a fast figure that ascends pedalling off the open G string. This lick concludes with some fast Dorian/pentatonic ideas at bar 83-86. Joe modulates again at bar 87, into the key of F♯ Dorian (F♯, G♯, A, B, C♯, D♯, E, F♯). This section includes more fast Dorian/pentatonic lines. Joe rounds off the solo with some bluesy ideas based around D Mixolydian (D, E, F♯, G, A, B, C, D), and E Mixolydian (E, F♯, G♯, A, B, C♯, D, E).

After another verse and extended chorus, there is a short breakdown section that enters at bar 145 and contains some fast legato phrases.

The song concludes with more Mixolydian lines and a bluesy riff that enters at bar 185 with the slide between the G and the A note being performed with the thumb over the top of the neck.

This track was recorded with an Ibanez guitar through either a Marshall or Soldano amp.

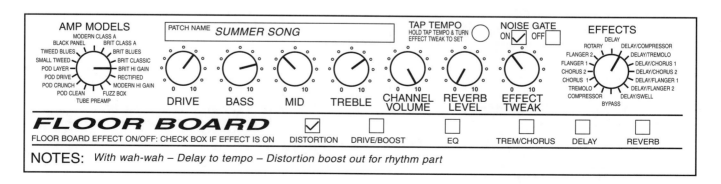

CRYIN'

This beautiful ballad can be found on the *Extremist* album, and features some of Joe's most soulful playing to date. The melody kicks off with soulful bends, and pre-bends using notes from E major pentatonic (E, F#, G#, B, C#, E). Accurate pitching of the bends is vital in performing this song correctly. The melody also includes lines based on the modes diatonic to E major (E, F#, G#, A, B, C#, D#, E). In places, Joe lets the notes sustain into feedback and also phrases passages slightly behind the beat, giving a laid back feel. At bar 9 Joe repeats the melody an octave higher and includes muted notes between the phrases. At bar 26 the whole band enters, with Joe playing some lower register major pentatonic lines. These gradually climb up the neck to climax with a wrenching blues line at bar 33. Joe then returns to the second half of the main theme found in the intro.

The solo enters at bar 43 with Joe playing phrases based around E minor pentatonic (E, G, A, B, D, E), and the E blues scale (E, G, A, Bb, B, D, E). Bar 47 introduces a melody based around C# Aeolian, (C#, D#, E, F#, G#, A, B, C#), that modulates to E Lydian (E, F#, G#, A#, B, C#, D, #E) over the F#/E chord. The solo section concludes with a short passage based around C# Aeolian and A Lydian over the arpeggiated C#m7add11 and A major7 chords. This section includes some smooth legato phrasing.

After returning to the main theme for the last time, Satch launches into a wrenching solo based around E minor pentatonic and the E blues scale. Satch really goes for it here, and allows open strings to ring between licks for a dramatic effect.

This track was recorded with an Ibanez guitar through a Zoom multi effects unit.

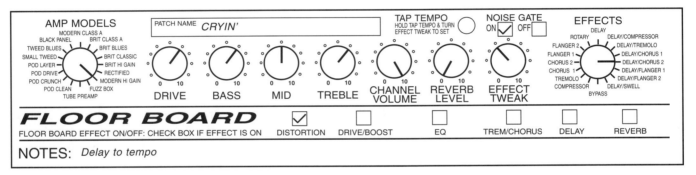

ALWAYS WITH ME, ALWAYS WITH YOU

This classic ballad can also be found on the *Surfing* album, and kicks off with some clean chord arpeggios, diatonic to the key of B major. The part uses slight palm muting and chorus. The Badd4 chord is pretty tricky, due to the wide stretching involved. The main melody enters at bar 17, and uses notes from the B major scale (B, C#, D#, E, F#, G#, A#, B). The melody makes use of some great phrasing, with fast slides into the notes. Satch also makes use of strong chord tones throughout the melody.

The solo kicks off at bar 48, with the rhythm guitar being embellished with a clean Nashville strung electric. During this section Satch employs the pitch axis technique, using B as an axis point between B major for the verse and B Aeolian for the solo (B, C#, D, E, F#, G, A, B). Satch demonstrates his soulful bends, plus more fluid legato phrasing in bar 54.

The main theme is reintroduced at bar 71, and is played an octave higher than in the verse. From bar 88, a two-handed tapping passage enters and uses the open B string as a pedal tone. This section concludes with some sliding double stops. The song concludes with more B major lines plus the main theme, and finishes with another legato line.

This track was probably recorded with an Ibanez guitar and a Rockman preamp.

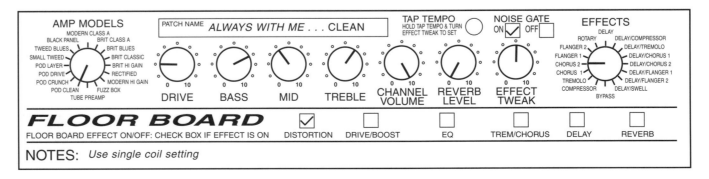

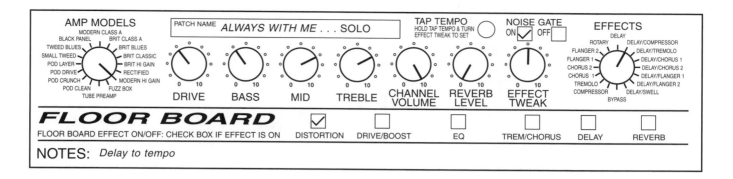

NOTES: *Delay to tempo*

SATCH BOOGIE

Another track from the classic *Surfing with the Alien* album, which clocks in with a tempo of 224 bpm, and should be performed with a fast swing shuffle feel. The intro is pretty tricky, and is based around A minor pentatonic (A, C, D, E, G, A), the A blues scale (A, C, D, E♭, E, G, A), and A mixolydian (A, B, C♯, D, E, F♯, G, A). The intro fuses fast single note lines with dominant triad ideas that result in a truly memorable intro. The intro concludes with a wrenching harmonic fretted at the 14th fret of the G string.

The main solo kicks off at bar 30, against a fast, bluesy, boogie rhythm part, and uses notes from A minor pentatonic, A blues, and A Dorian (A, B, C, D, E, F♯, G, A). The solo includes classic blues phrasing, with some aggressive fast licks. A section based around D mixolydian is introduced at bar 45, and uses plenty of left hand slurs and position shifts. At bar 53 a fast legato line is performed based around F♯ Aeolian (F♯, G♯, A, B, C♯, D, E, F♯). This is followed by a screaming harmonic performed just past the second fret. The A5 riff is re-introduced at bar 61, and Satch continues to blast out rapid blues licks. Bar 69 includes a fast tapped section, with the tapped notes being produce by striking the string with the edge of the pick. The verse concludes with some diatonic sixth ideas, embellished with double stops, plus some fast runs based around F♯ minor pentatonic (F♯, A, B, C♯, E, F♯).

The final section of the song is introduced at bar 97, and demonstrates Satch's use of pitch axis. This is where one note is used as an axis to other scales. Here Joe uses the open A string to modulate into a variety of different keys, using two-handed tapping. This section also uses a heavy flanging effect. The song concludes with the intro riff.

This song was probably recorded with an Ibanez guitar through a Marshall amp.

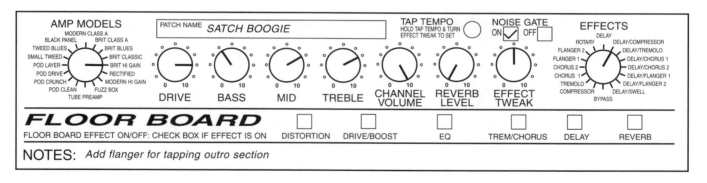

NOTES: *Add flanger for tapping outro section*

CIRCLES

Another track from *Surfing with the Alien*, this track kicks off with a clean rhythm passage based around E minor. The part includes a muted low E to keep the 16th note rhythm moving. The guitar sound includes chorus and a rhythmic digital delay.

The main solo kicks in at bar 23, with a heavy dose of distortion and wah. Satch starts out in familiar territory, using E minor pentatonic (E, G, A, B, D, E). Bar 27 introduces a long two-handed tapped section, also based around E minor pentatonic, that also includes the B♭ note from the E blues scale (E, G, A, B♭, B, D, E), via slides with the tapping hand. Another long tapping/legato passage appears at bar 35, using both E minor pentatonic and E Dorian (E, F♯, G, A, B, C♯, D, E). Bar 39 modulates to the key of A minor, and kicks off with a sweep-picked A minor arpeggio, plus a fast figure based around A Aeolian (A,

B, C, D, E, F, G, A). The final section of the solo uses notes from B Mixolydian (B, C♯, D♯, E, F♯, G♯, A, B), over the B7 chord plus diatonic lines over D7 and C major7 from the key of G major. The solo concludes with some whammy dives and harmonic.

The song concludes with the clean intro guitar riff. This song was probably recorded with an Ibanez guitar and a Rockman preamp.

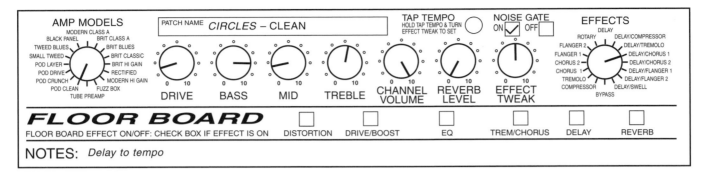

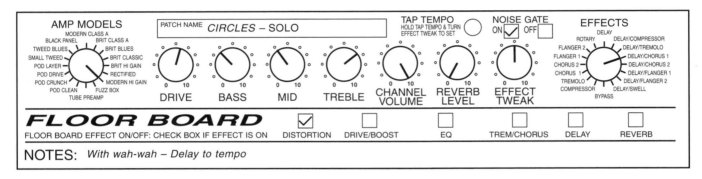

THE EXTREMIST

The title cut from the album of the same name, this track kicks off with a riff played on a Nashville-tuned Dobro guitar. All of the guitars on this track were tuned a semi-tone lower than concert pitch for extra weight. The main electric riff enters at the end of bar 4, with plenty of valve crunch and live reverb. The main riff is based is based around E Dorian (E, F♯, G, A, B, C♯, D, E). The melody kicks in at bar 13 and includes bluesy double stops and lines based around E Dorian and E minor pentatonic (E, G, A, B, D, E). The chorus enters at bar 21, with some ascending unison bends that outline the chords.

After the harmonica solo (played by Joe!), the main solo enters at bar 33, with an ascending line using notes from C♯ Aeolian (C♯, D♯, E, F♯, G♯, A, B, C♯). The run includes open strings between the position shifts. More legato phrasing at bars 35-36 follows this. Joe includes some blues lines based around C♯ minor pentatonic (C♯, E, F♯, G♯, B, C♯). Bars 41-44 include more fast legato ideas that include lots of position shifts. After more blues ideas, the section concludes with a B Mixolydian pedal tone figure that uses the open B as the pedal tone. The solo concludes with some random harmonics found over the pickups. These are produced by the right hand as pinched harmonics, while the left hand operates the whammy bar. The final melody is based around the A Phrygian dominant mode (A, B♭, C♯, D, E, F, G, A).

The song concludes after another verse and chorus and a harmonic solo. This track was recorded with an Ibanez guitar through either a Marshall or a Soldano amp.

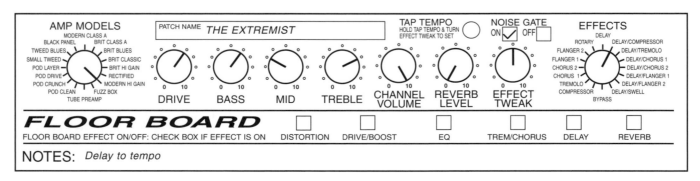

Guitar Notation Legend

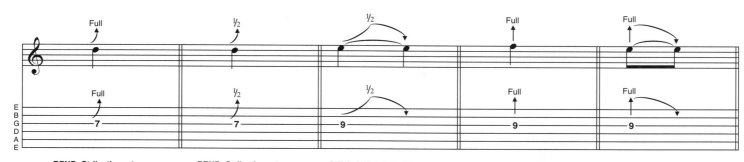

BEND: Strike the note and bend up a whole step (two frets).

BEND: Strike the note and bend up a half step (one fret).

BEND AND RELEASE: Strike the note, bend up a half step, then release the bend.

PRE-BEND: Bend the note up, then strike it.

PRE-BEND AND RELEASE: Bend up, strike the note, then release it.

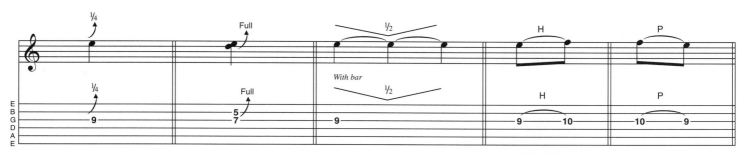

QUARTER-TONE BEND: Bend the note slightly sharp.

UNISON BEND: Strike both notes, then bend the lower note up to the pitch of the higher one.

TREMOLO BAR BENDS: Strike the note, and push the bar down and up by the amounts indicated.

HAMMER-ON: Strike the first note, then sound the second by fretting it without picking.

PULL-OFF: Strike the higher note, then pull the finger off while keeping the lower one fretted.

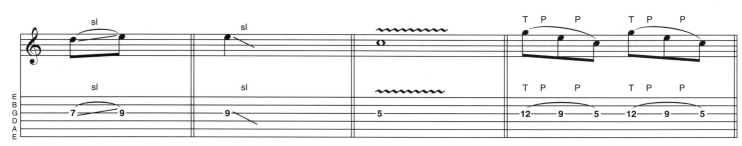

SLIDE: Slide the finger from the first note to the second. Only the first note is struck.

SLIDE: Slide to the fret from a few frets below or above.

VIBRATO: The string is vibrated by rapidly bending and releasing a note with the fretboard hand or tremolo bar.

TAPPING: Hammer on to the note marked with a T using the picking hand, then pull off to the next note, following the hammer-ons or pull-offs in the normal way.

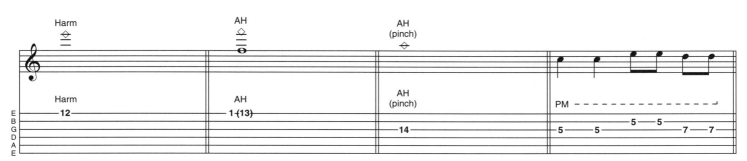

NATURAL HARMONIC: Lightly touch the string directly over the fret shown, then strike the note to create a "chiming" effect.

ARTIFICIAL HARMONIC: Fret the note, then use the picking hand finger to touch the string at the position shown in brackets and pluck with another finger.

ARTIFICIAL HARMONIC: The harmonic is produced by using the edge of the picking hand thumb to "pinch" the string whilst picking firmly with the plectrum.

PALM MUTES: Rest the palm of the picking hand on the strings near the bridge to produce a muted effect. Palm mutes can apply to a single note or a number of notes (shown with a dashed line).

Surfing With
The Alien

Music by
Joe Satriani

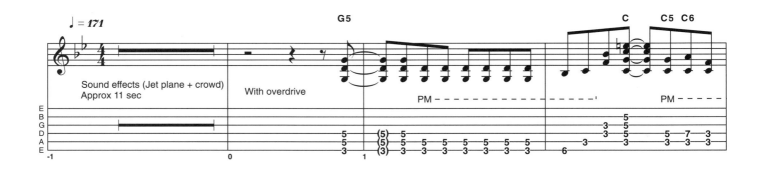

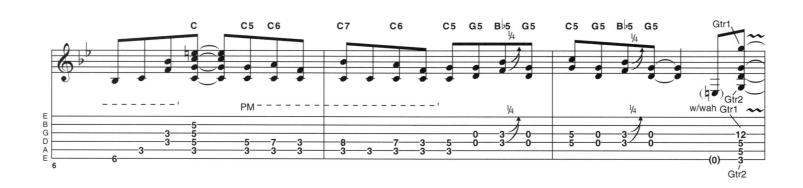

18

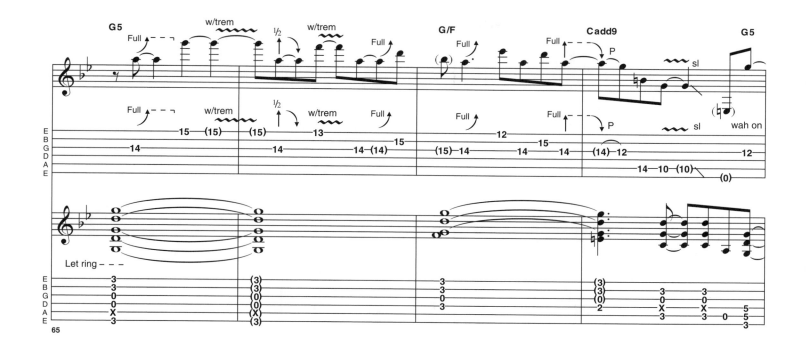

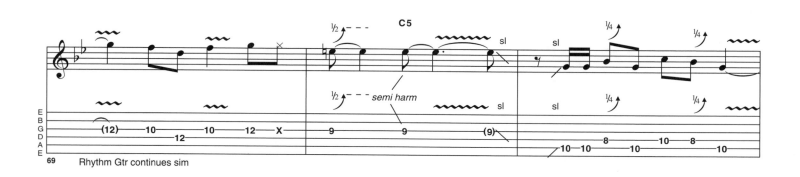

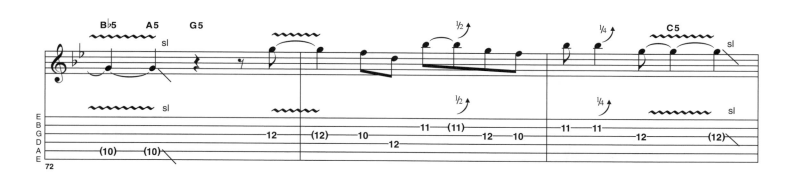

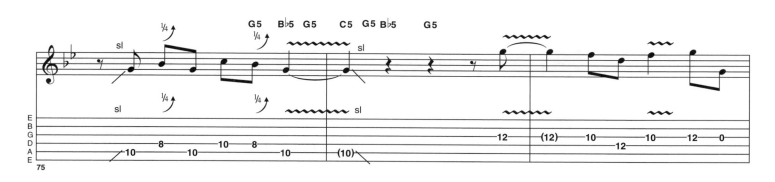

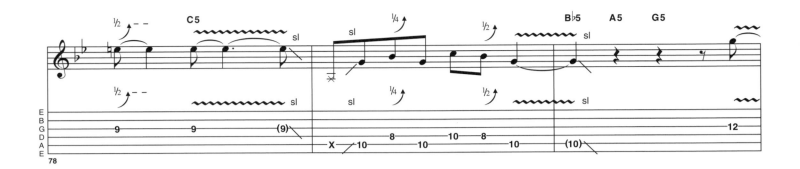

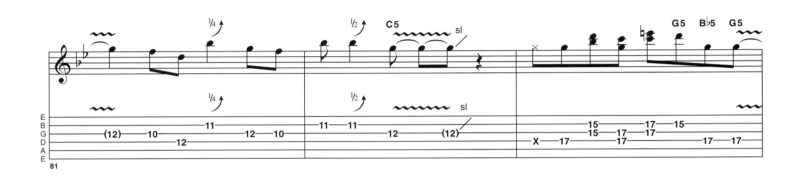

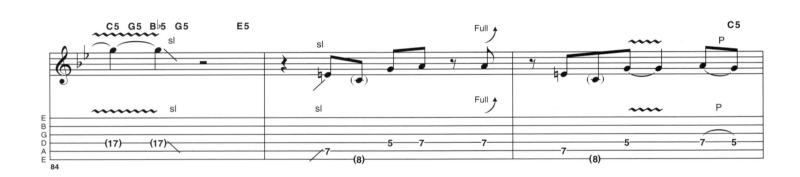

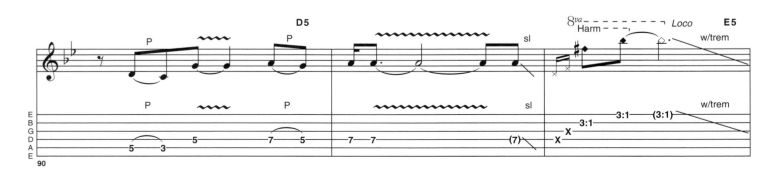

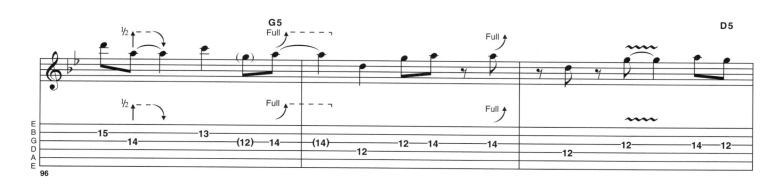

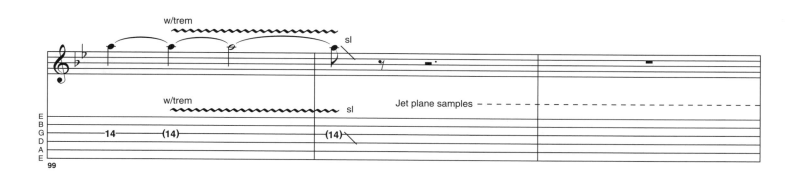

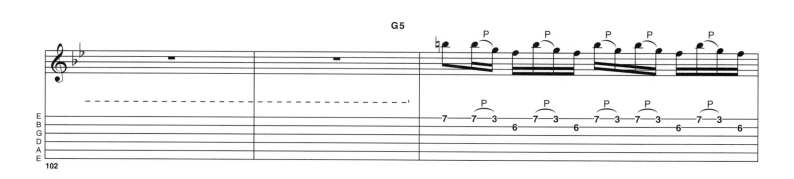

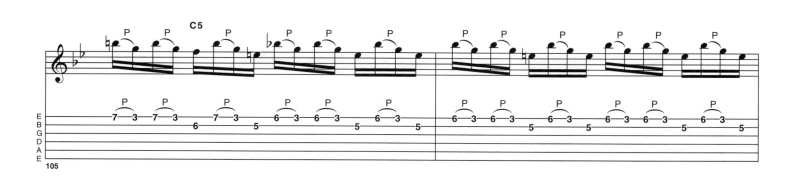

23

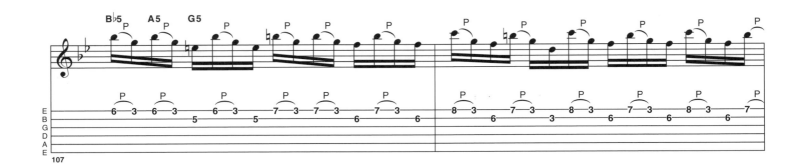

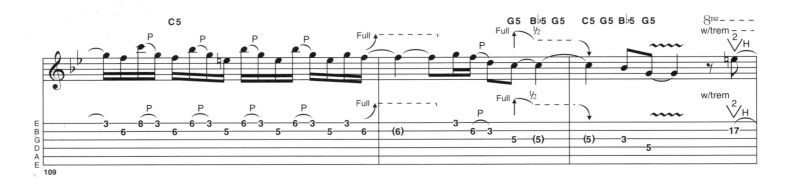

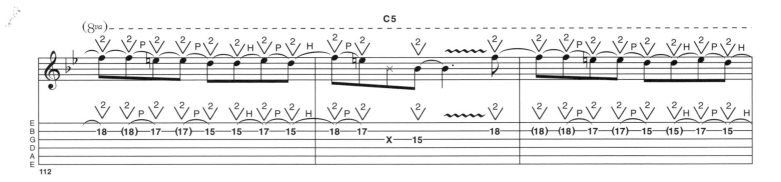

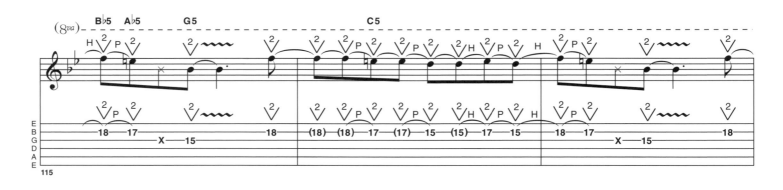

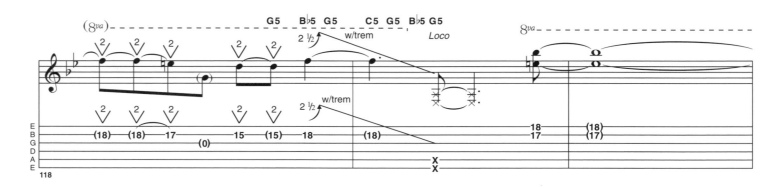

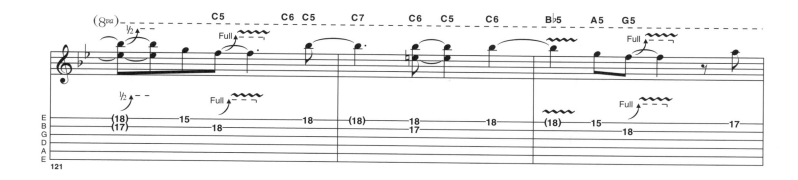

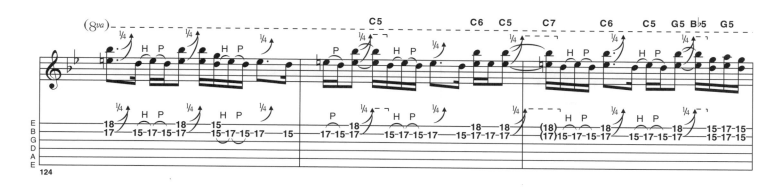

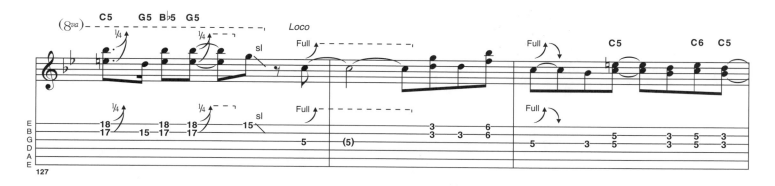

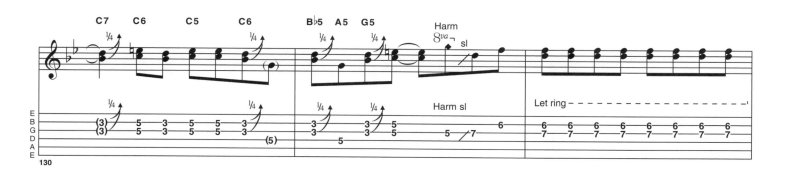

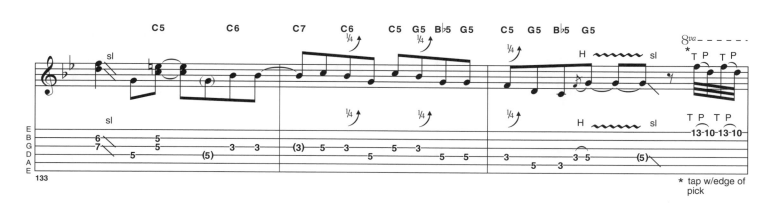

* tap w/edge of
pick

25

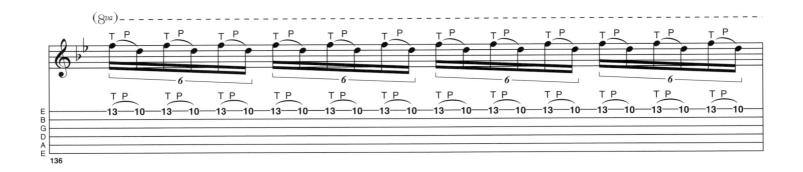

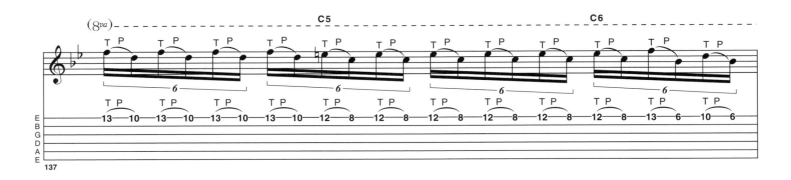

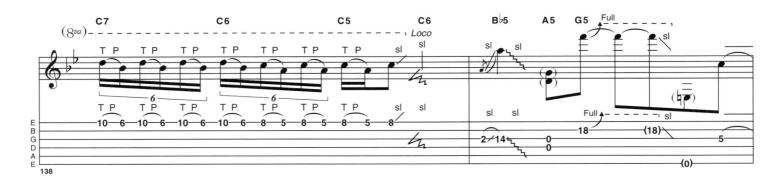

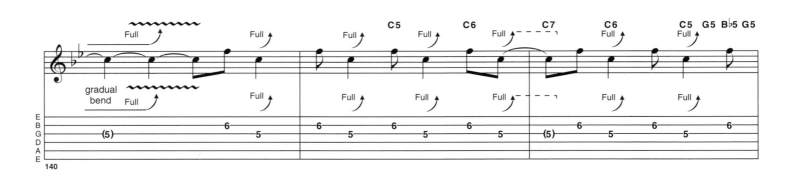

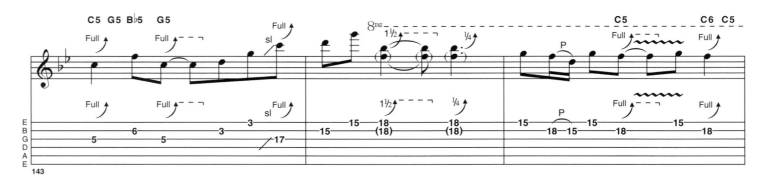

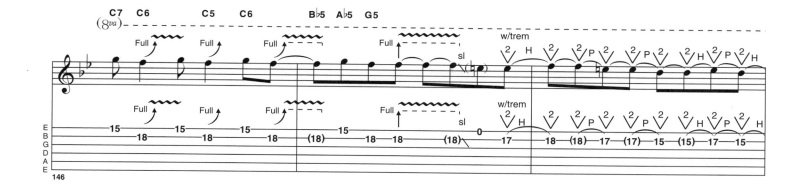

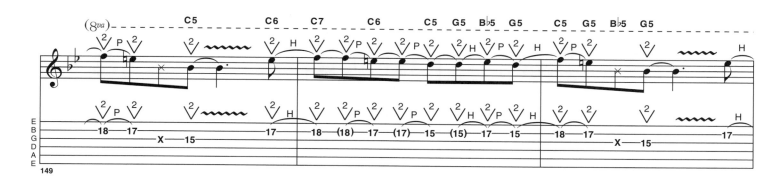

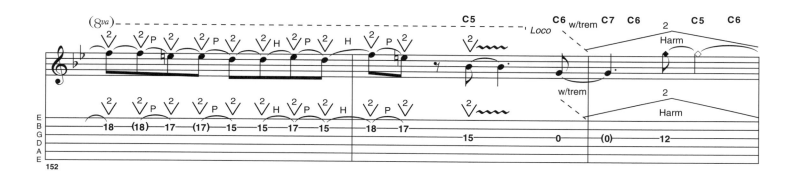

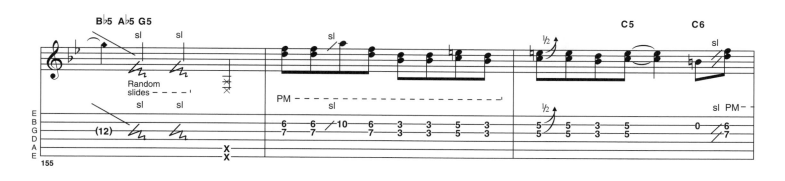

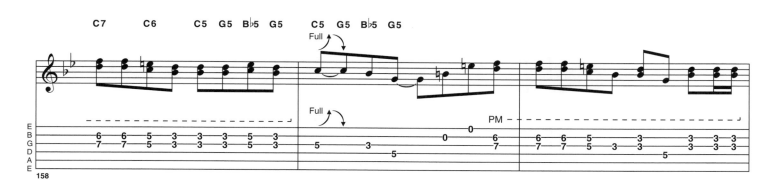

27

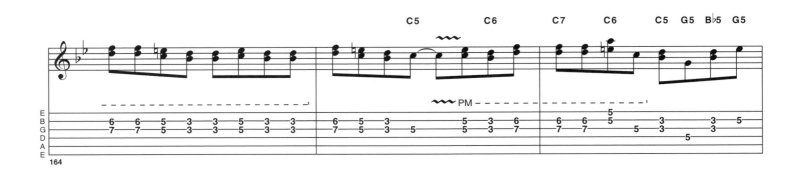

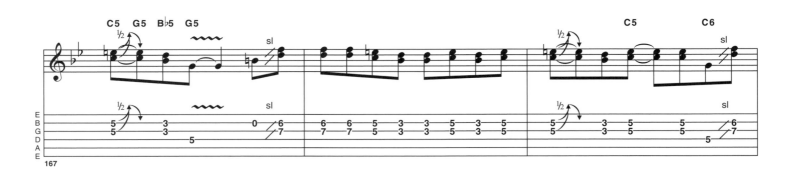

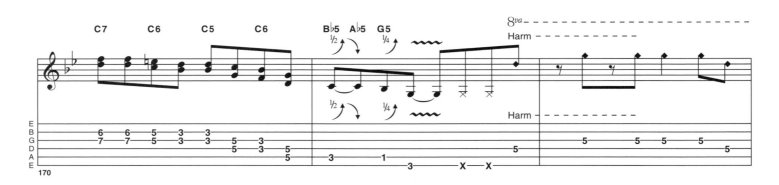

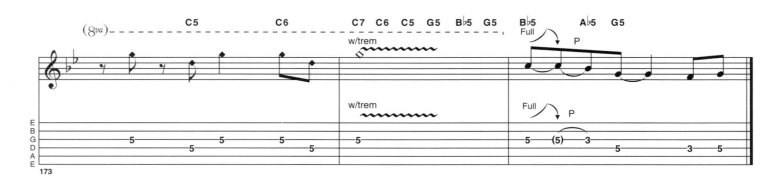

Flying In A Blue Dream

Music by
Joe Satriani

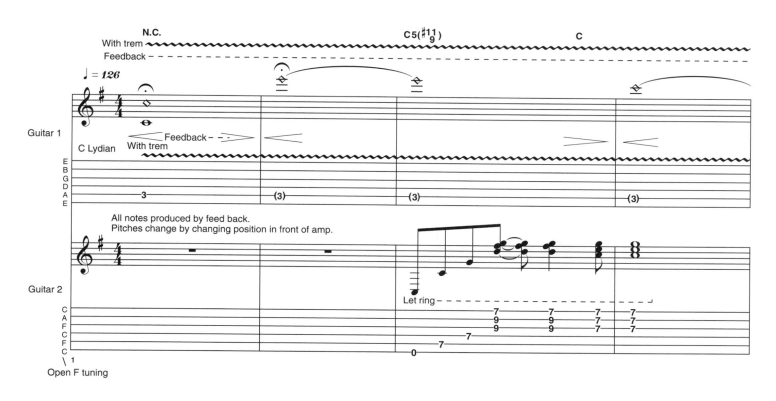

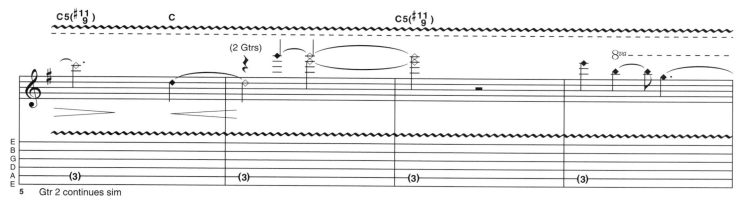

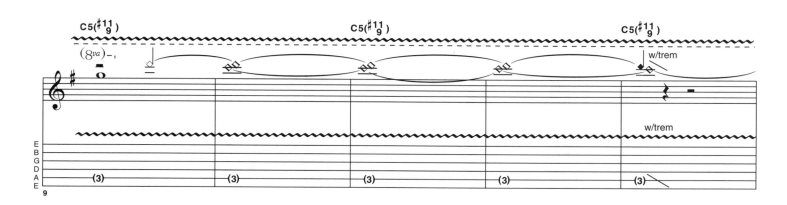

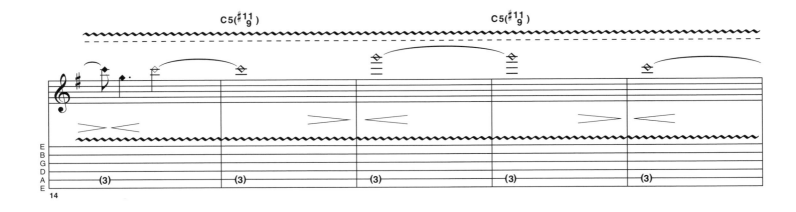

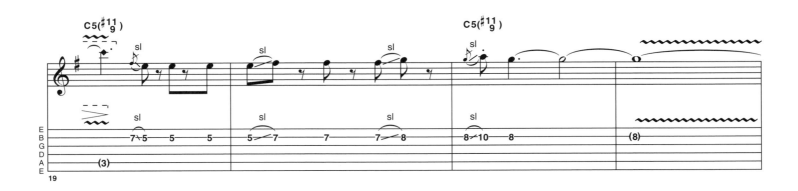

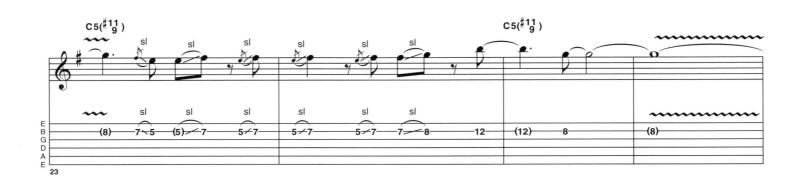

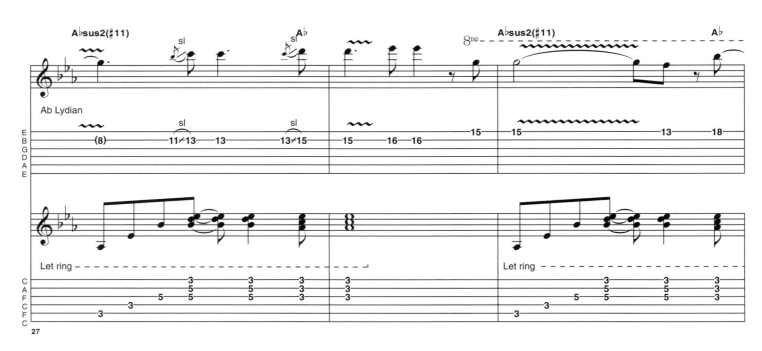

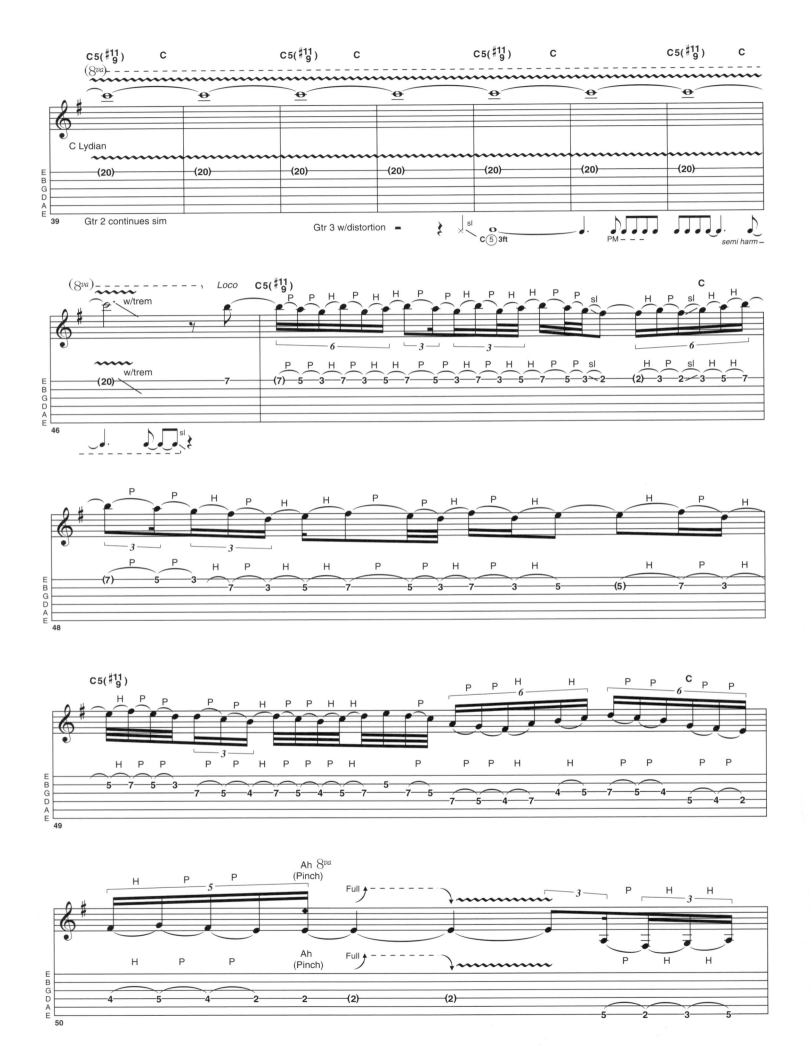

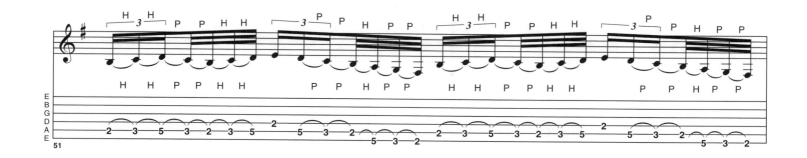

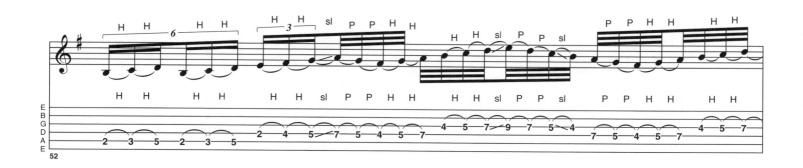

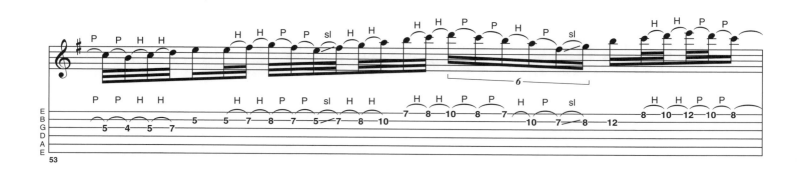

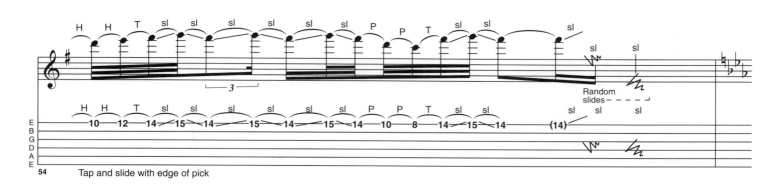

Tap and slide with edge of pick

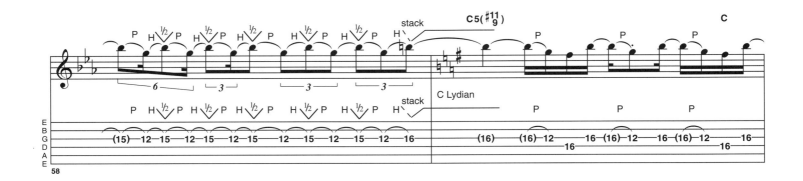

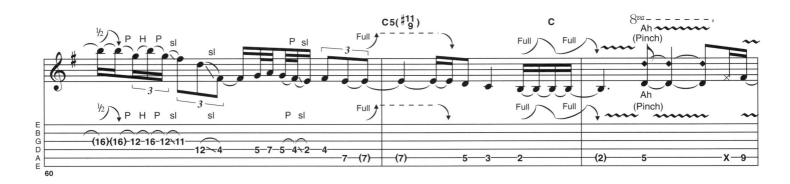

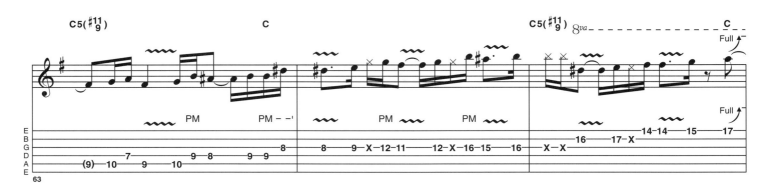

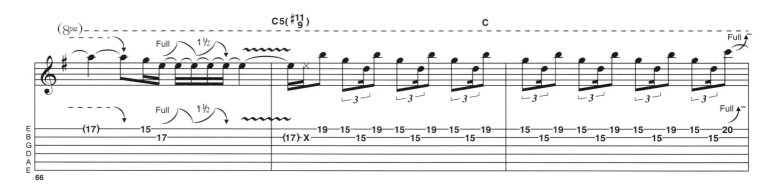

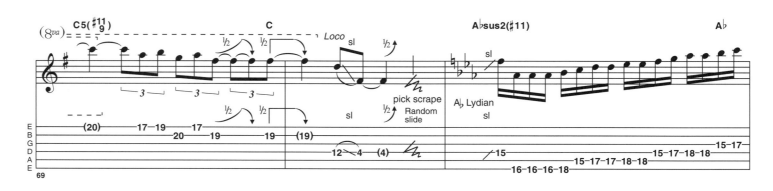

34

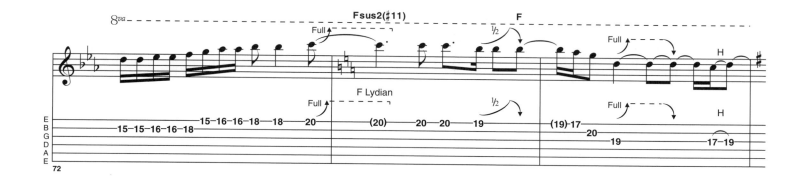

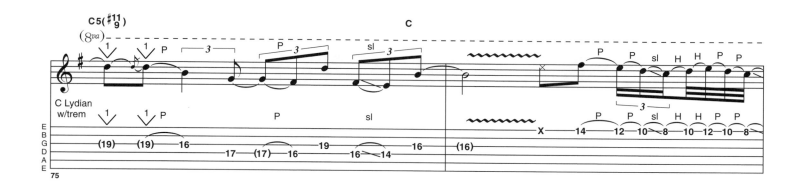

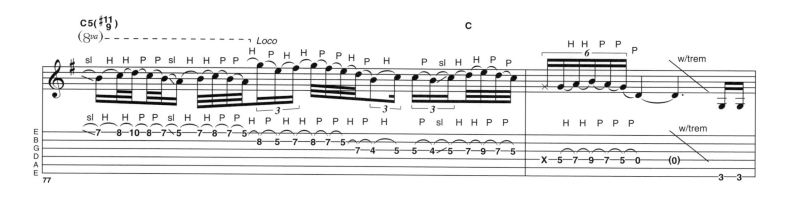

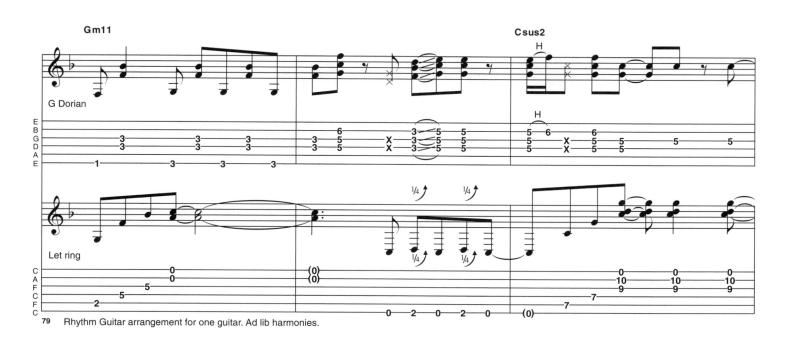

79 Rhythm Guitar arrangement for one guitar. Ad lib harmonies.

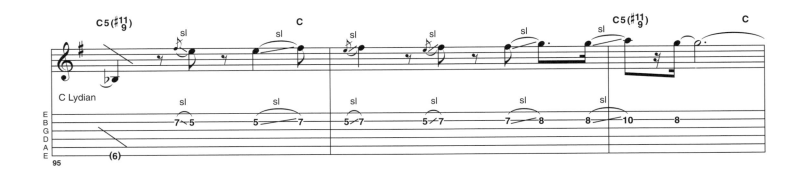

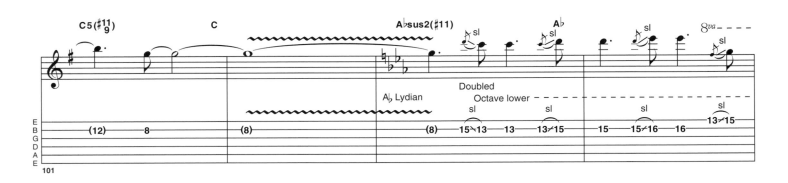

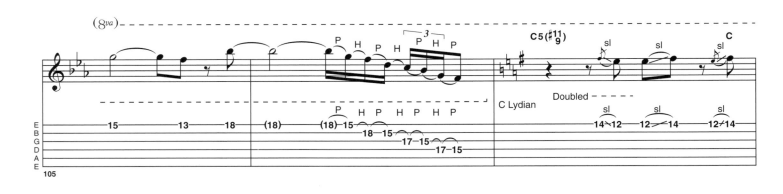

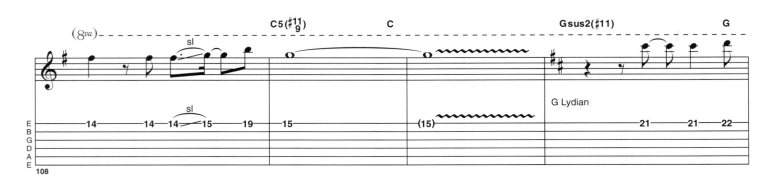

Summer Song

Music by
Joe Satriani

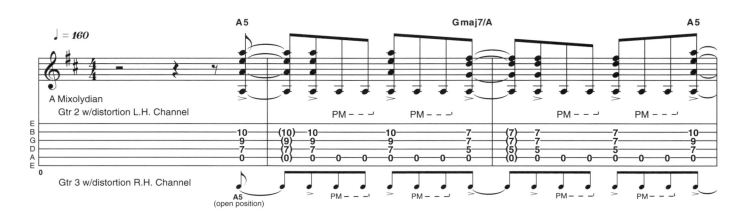

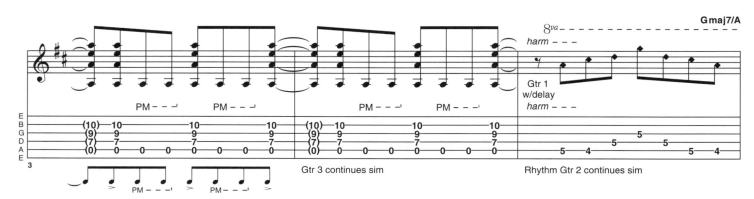

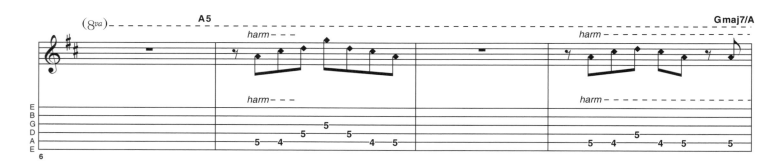

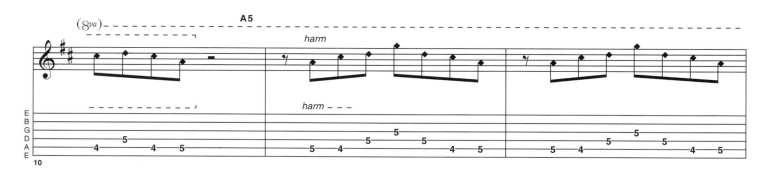

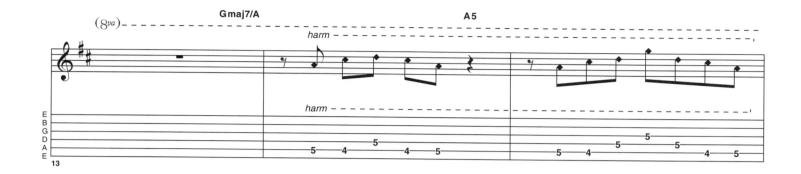

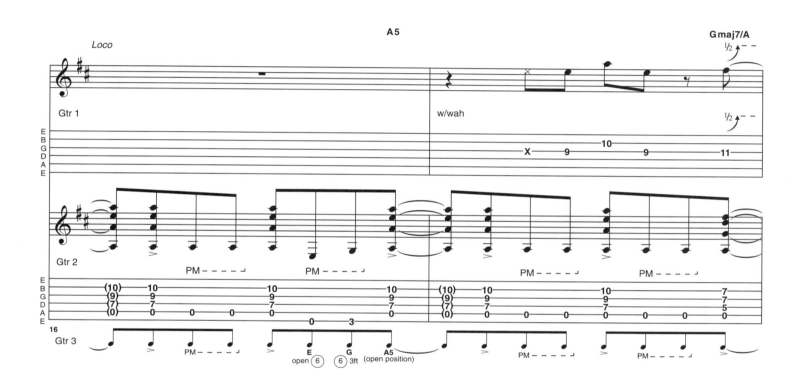

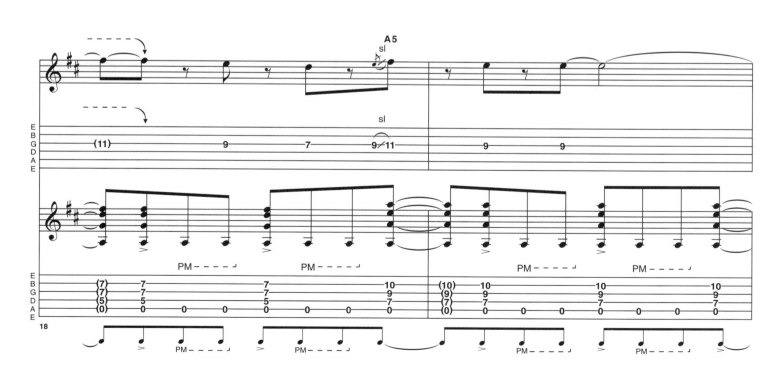

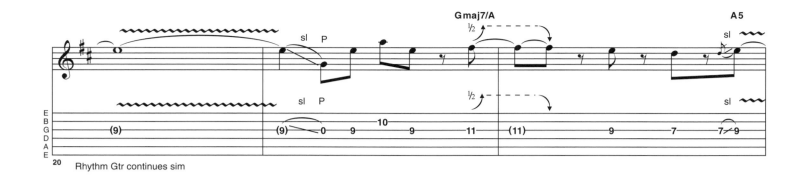

Rhythm Gtr continues sim

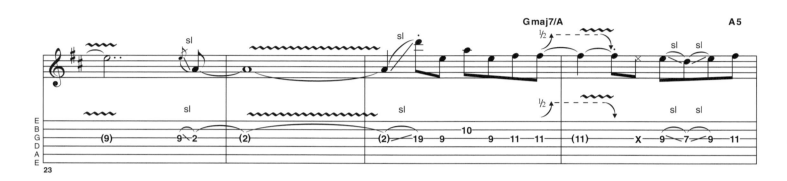

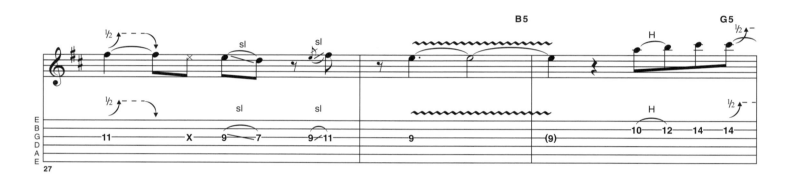

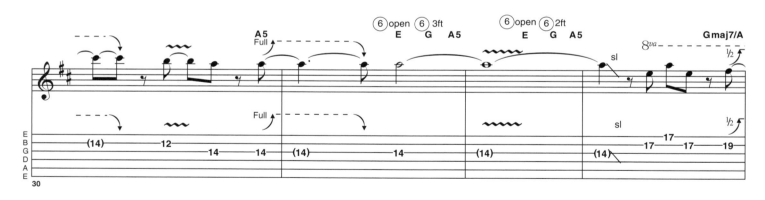

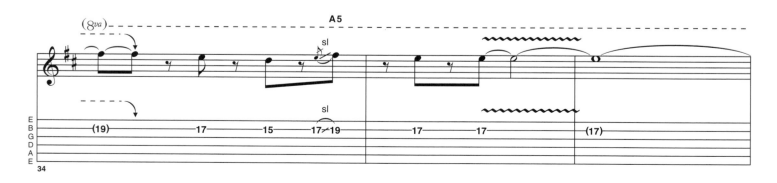

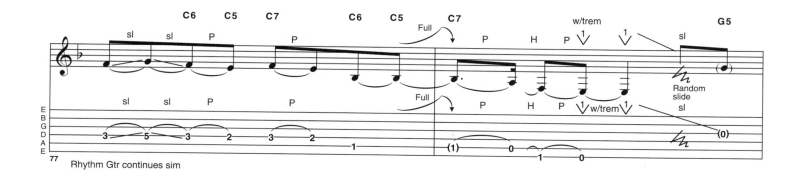

Rhythm Gtr continues sim

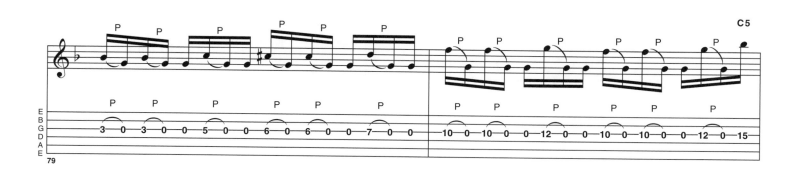

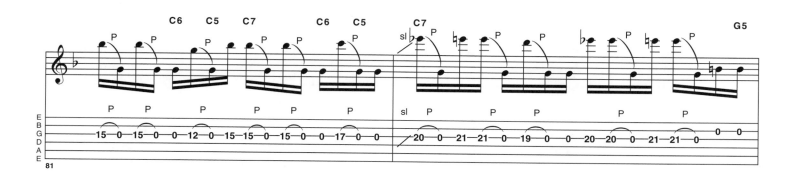

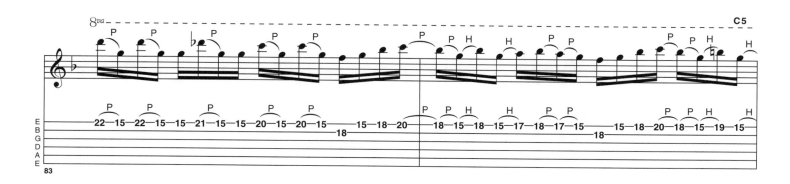

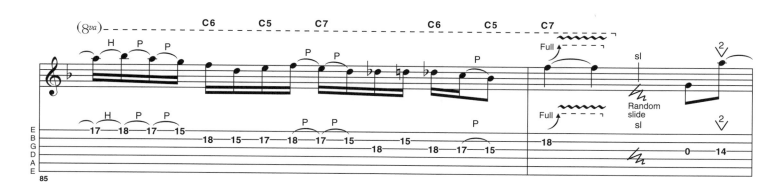

47

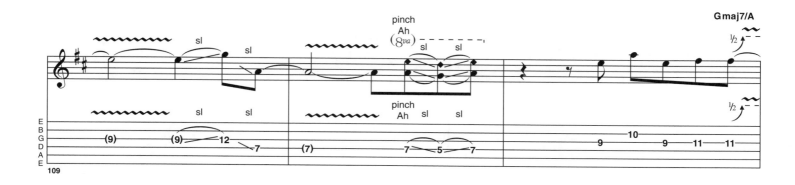

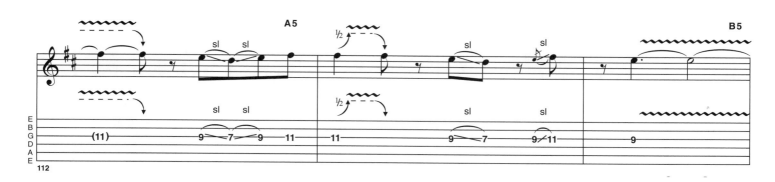

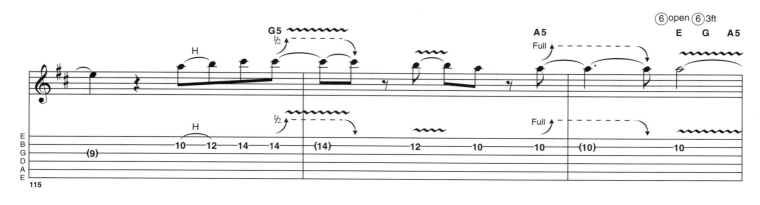

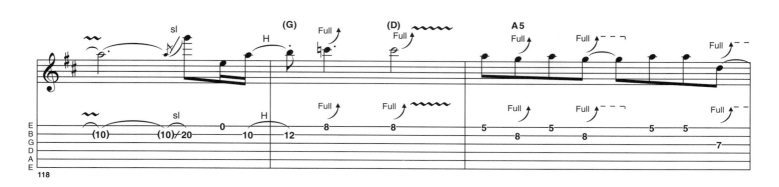

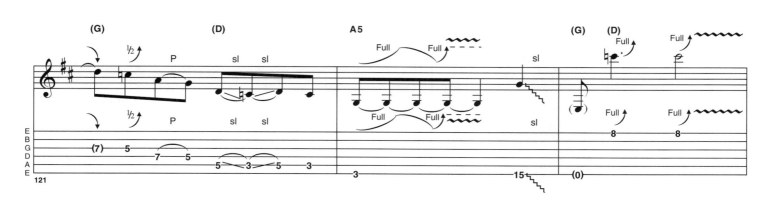

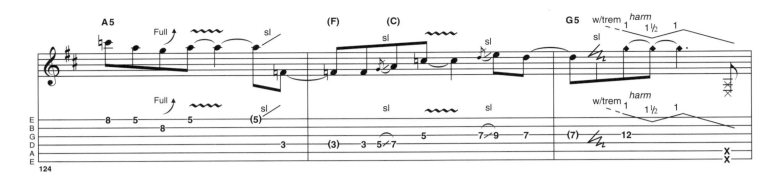

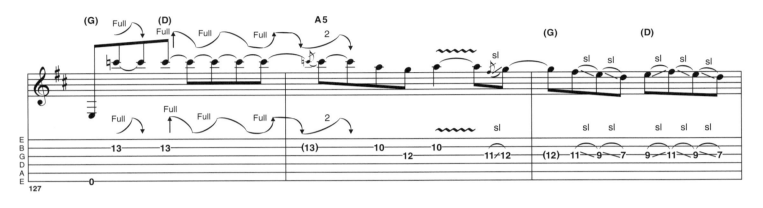

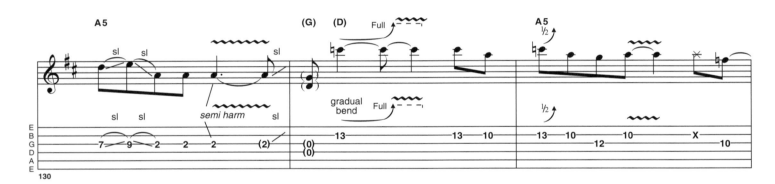

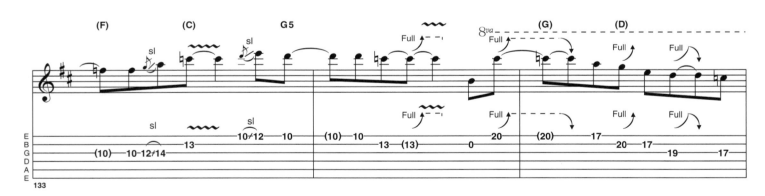

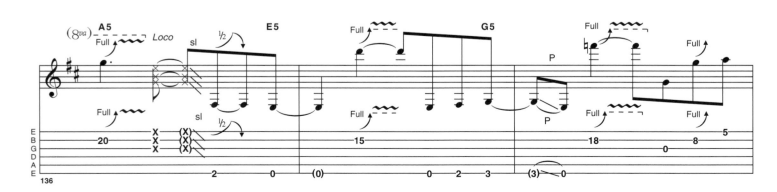

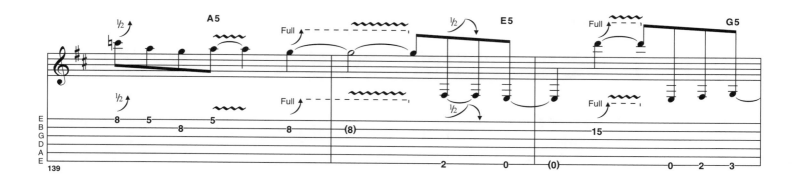

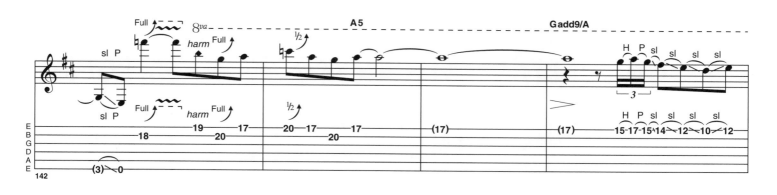

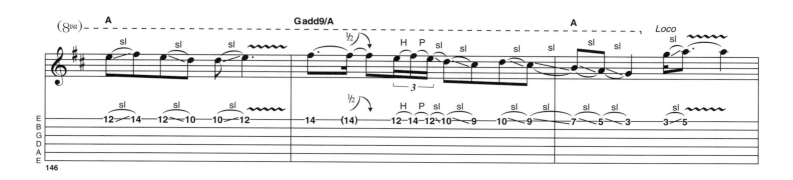

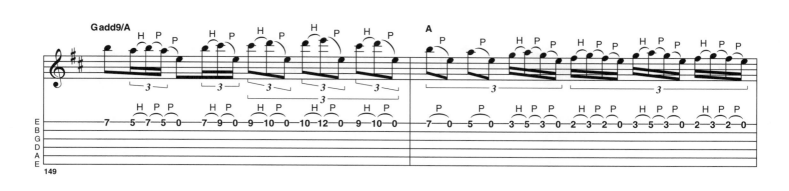

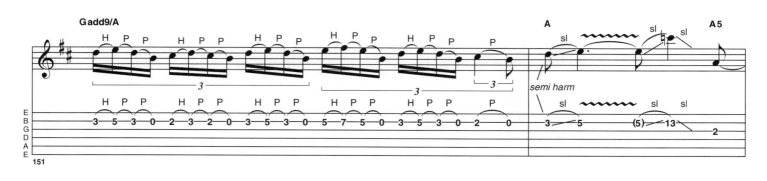

53

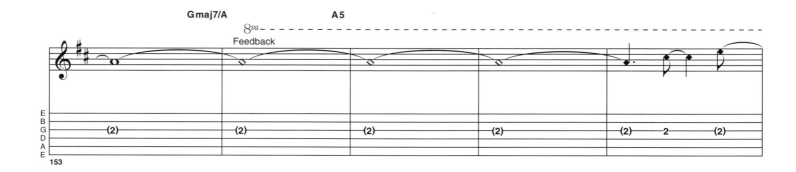

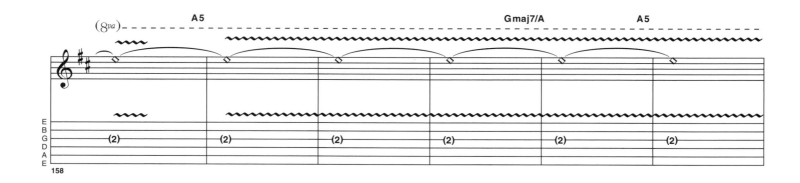

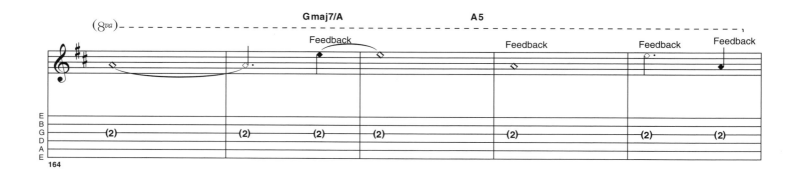

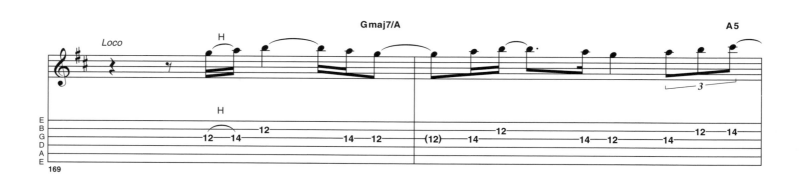

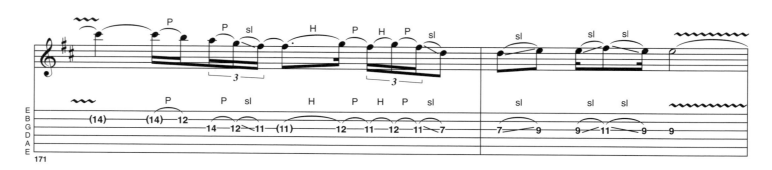

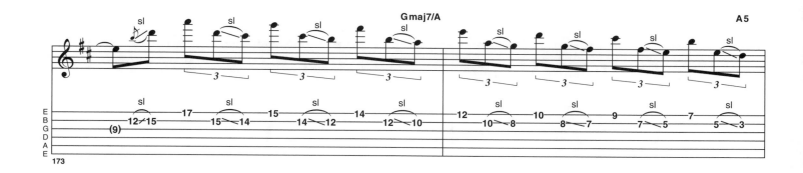

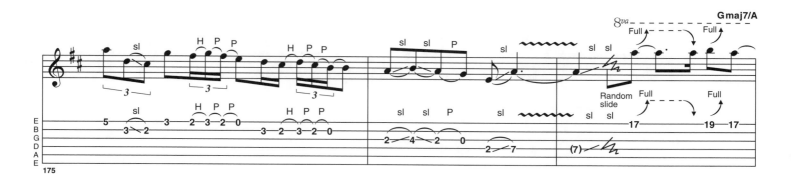

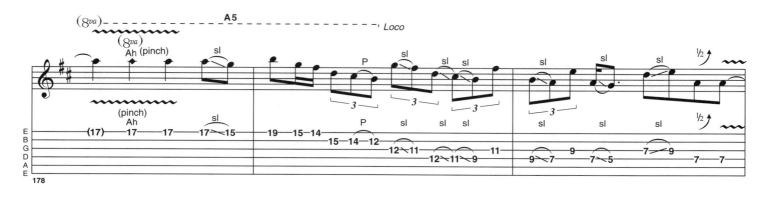

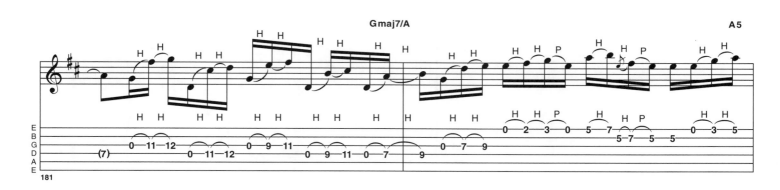

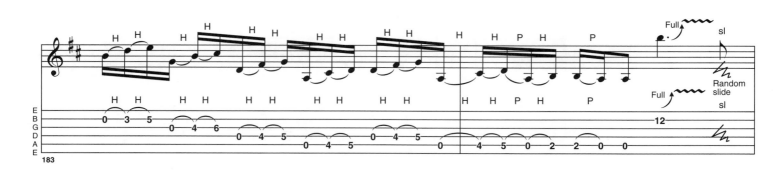

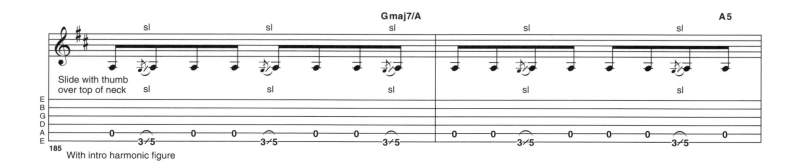

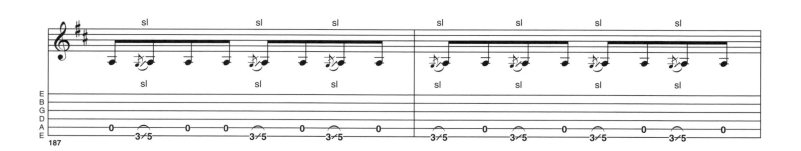

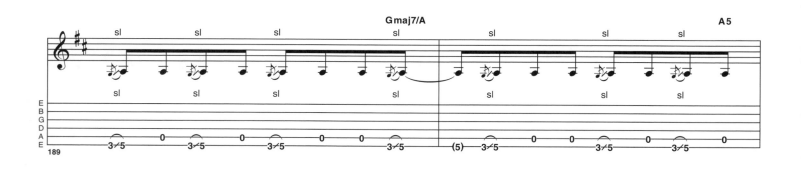

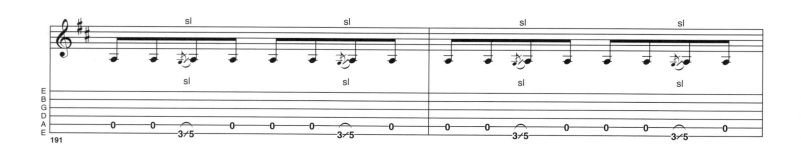

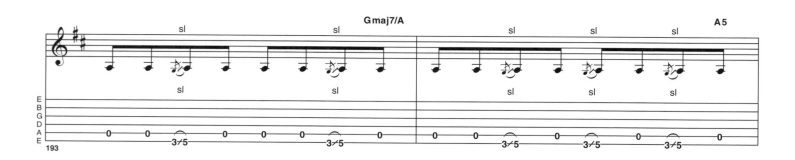

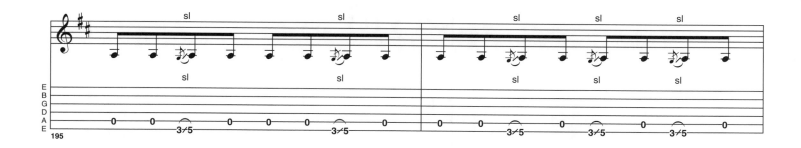

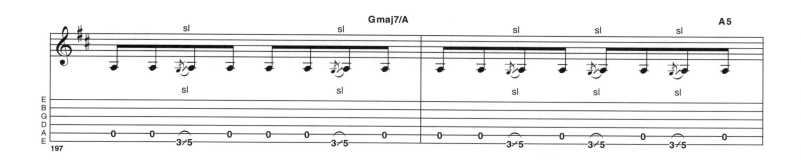

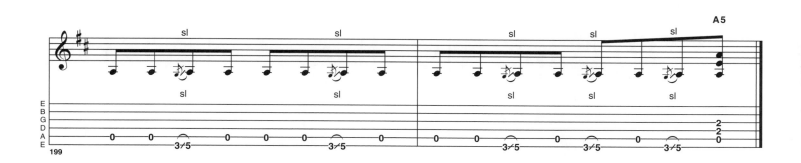

Cryin'

Music by
Joe Satriani

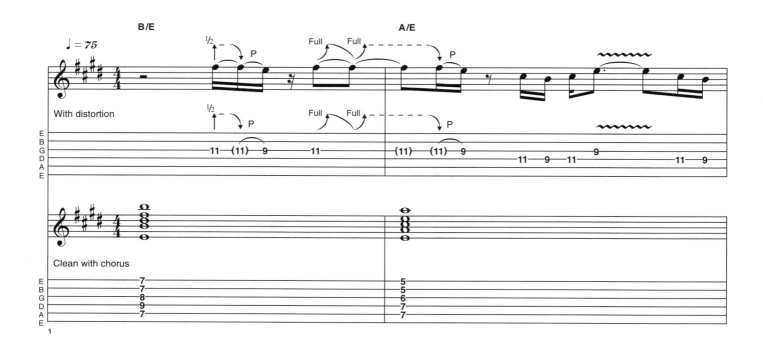

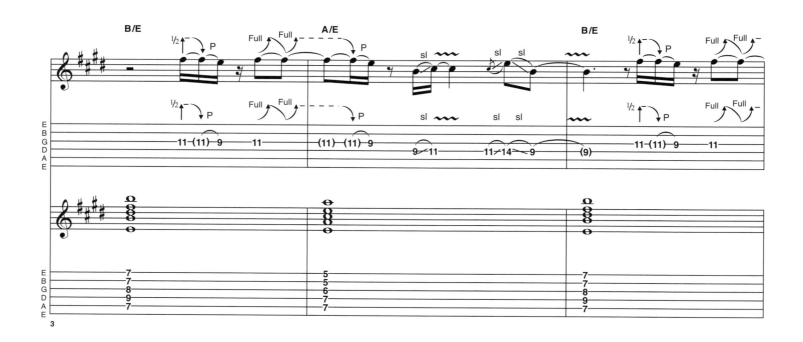

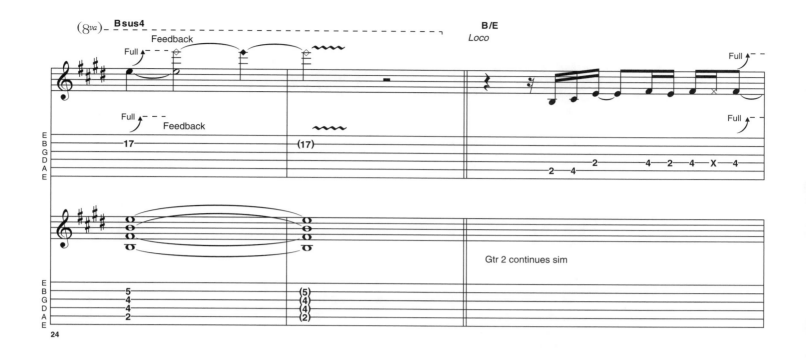

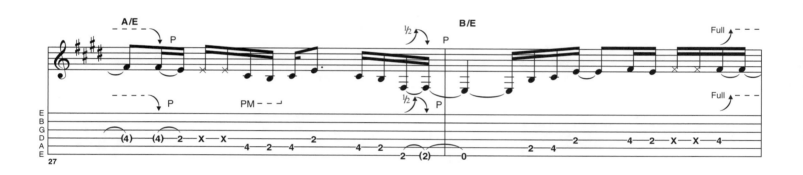

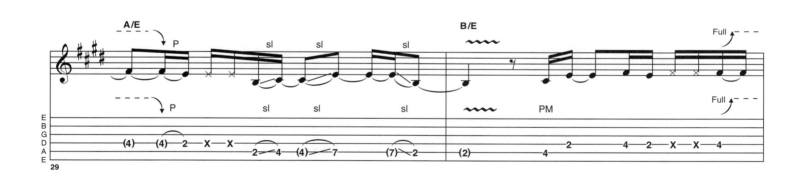

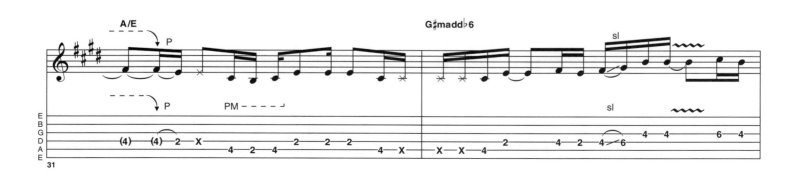

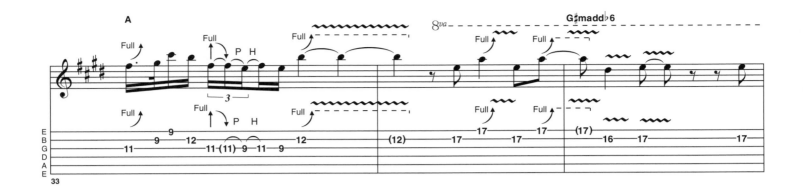

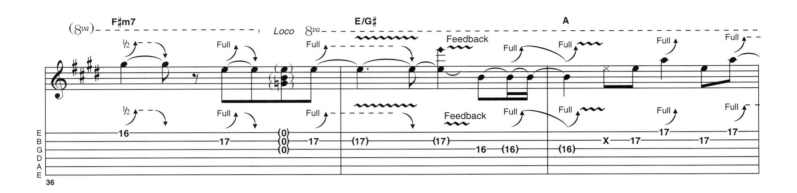

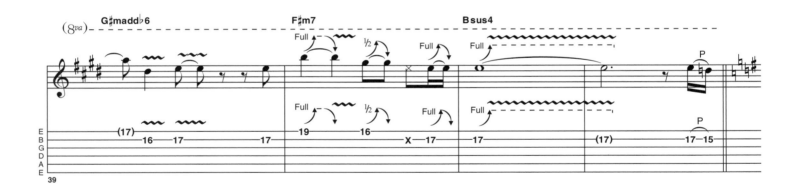

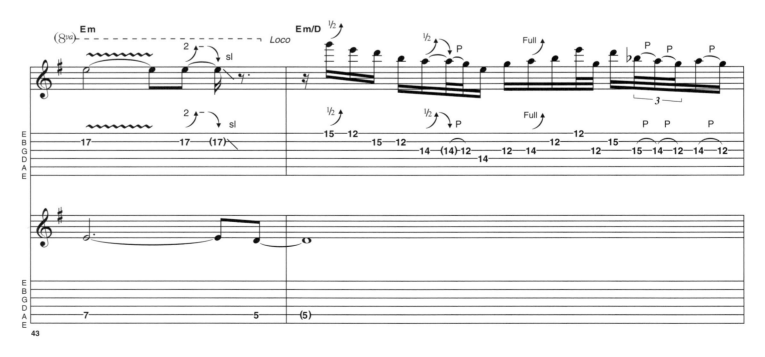

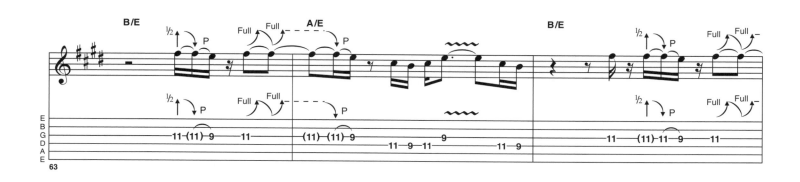

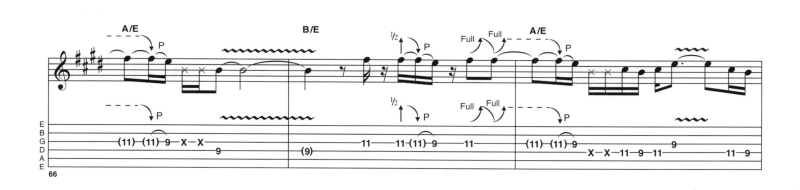

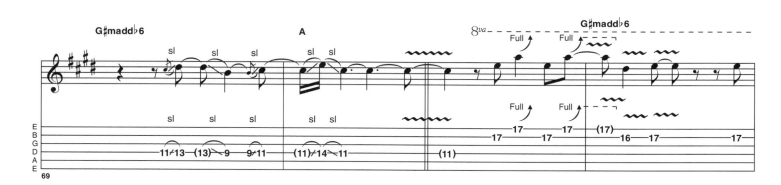

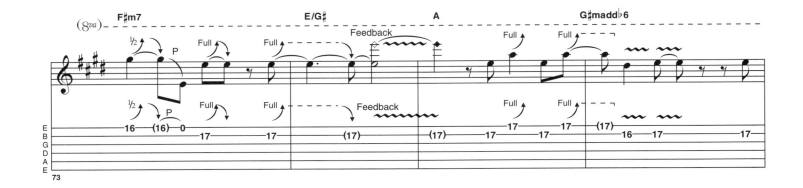

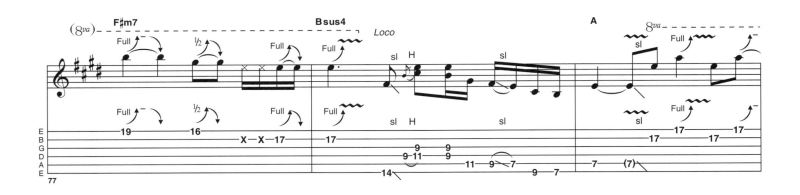

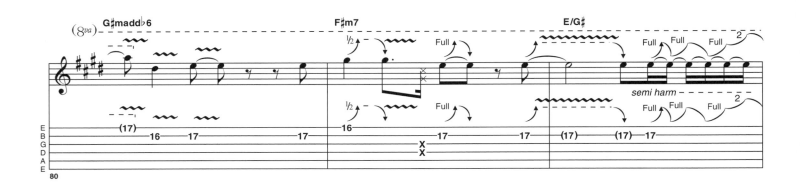

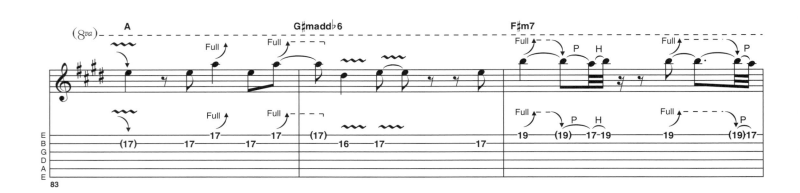

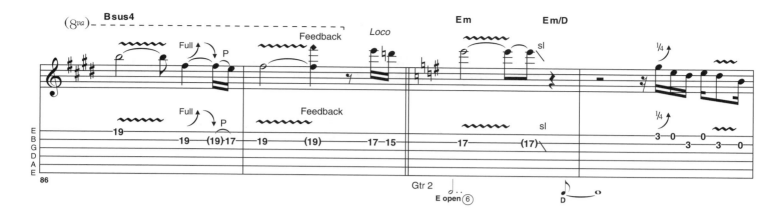

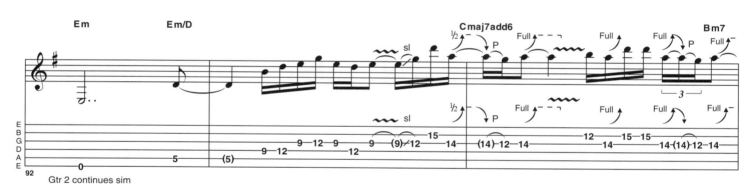

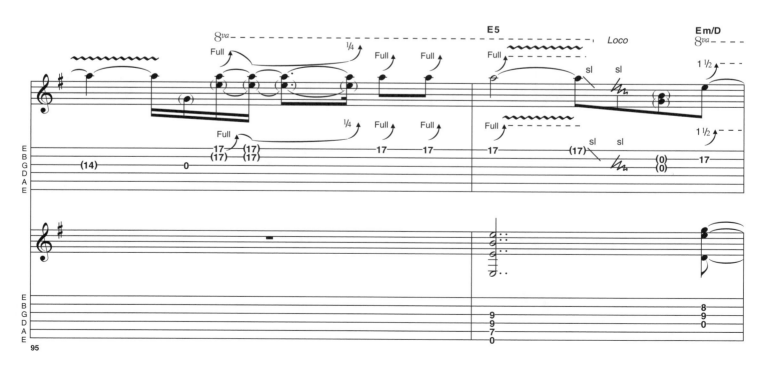

Always With Me, Always With You

Music by
Joe Satriani

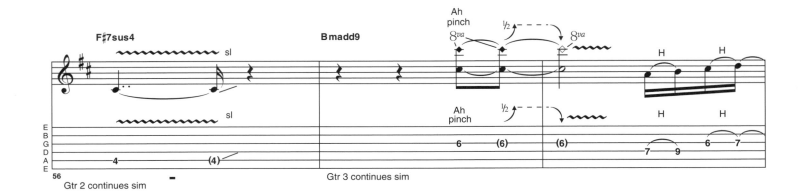

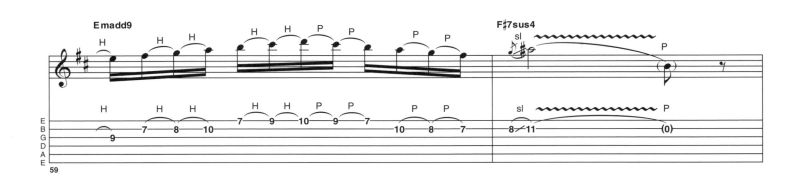

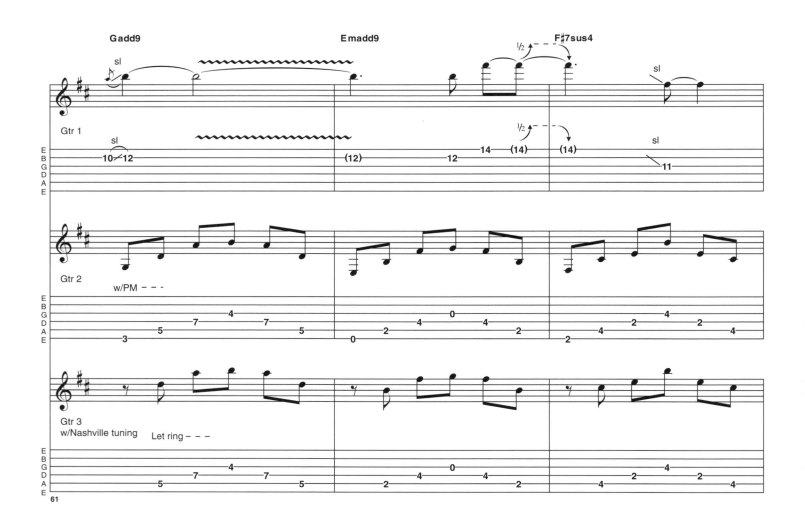

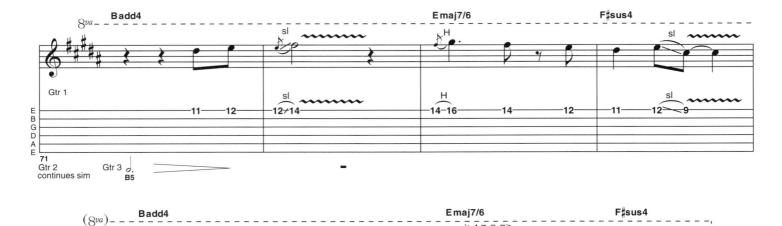

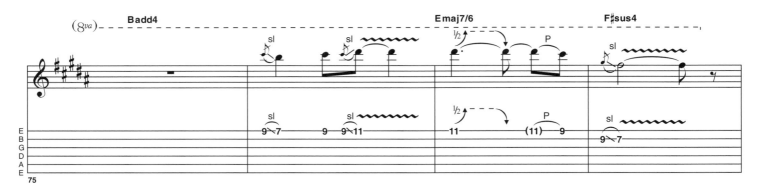

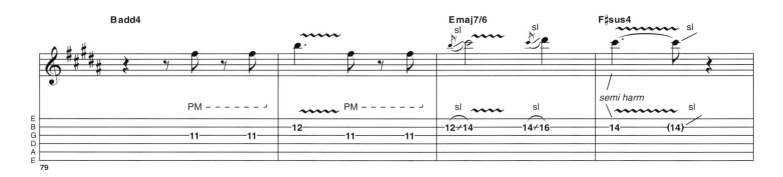

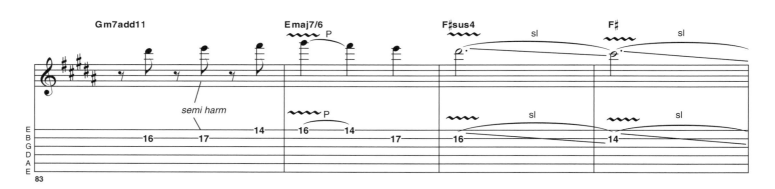

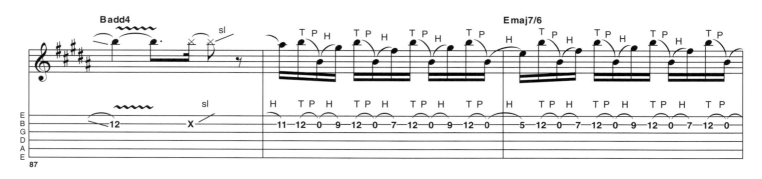

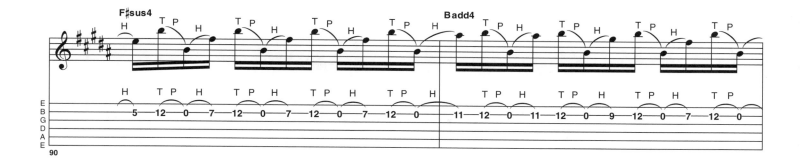

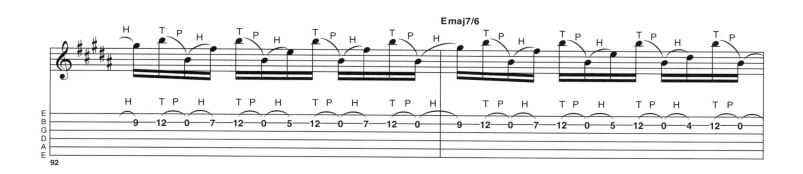

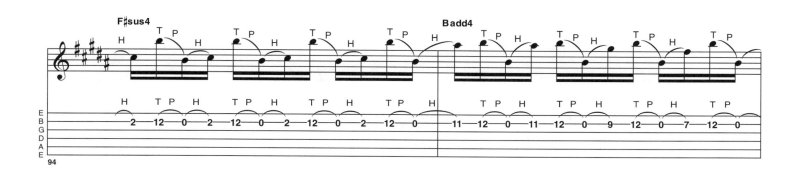

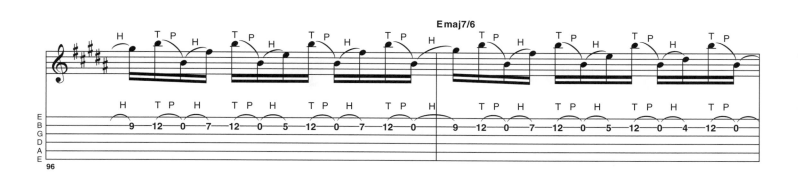

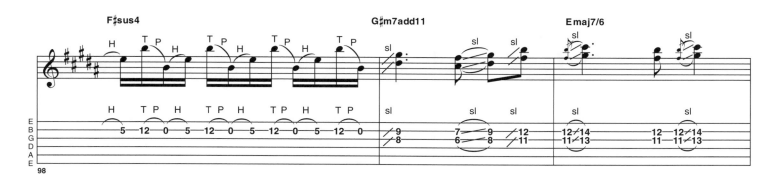

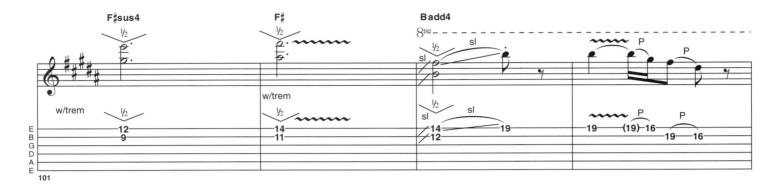

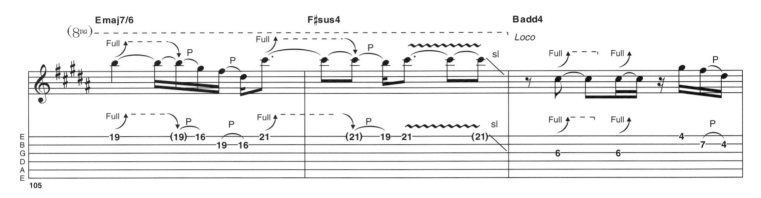

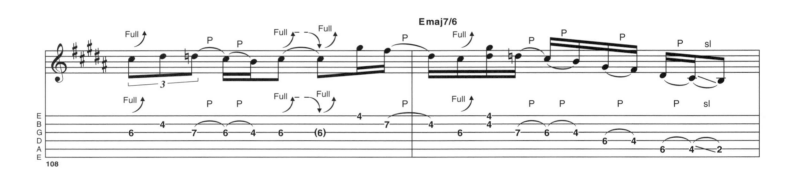

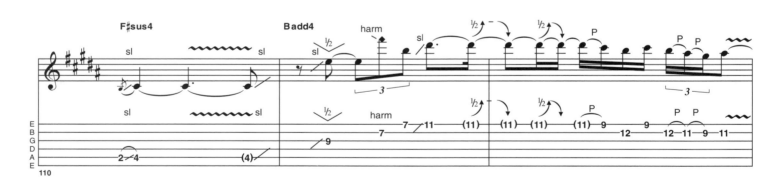

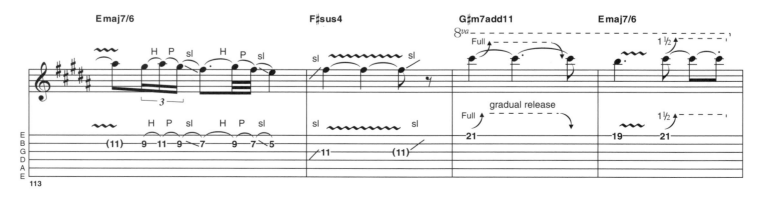

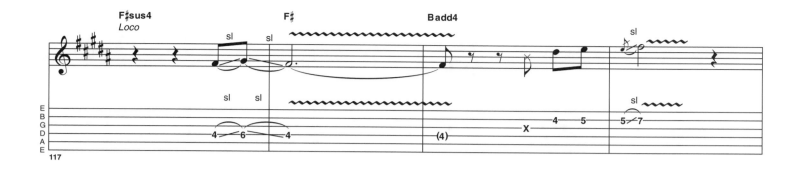

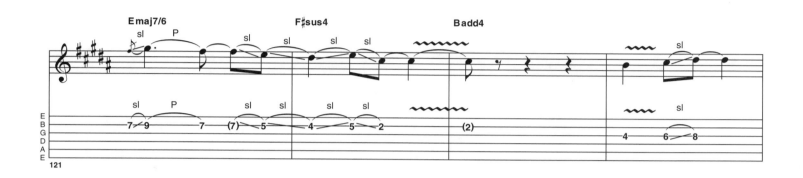

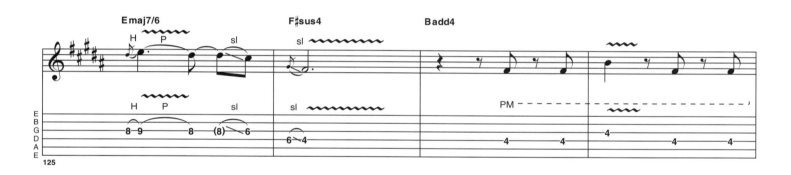

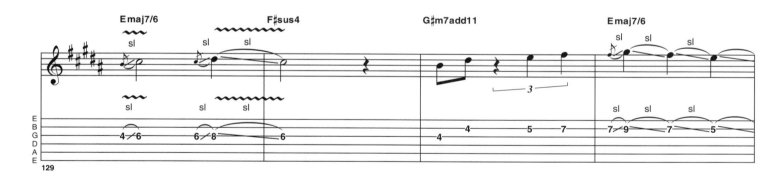

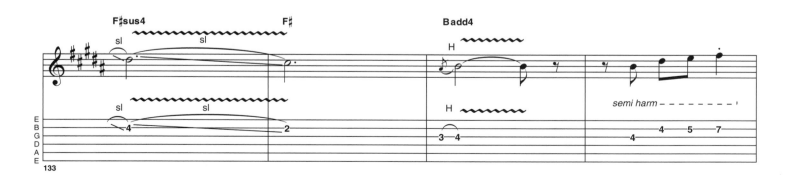

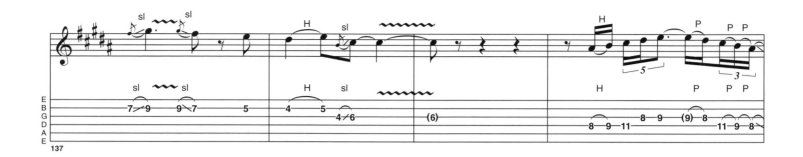

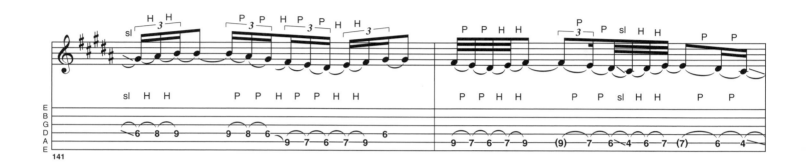

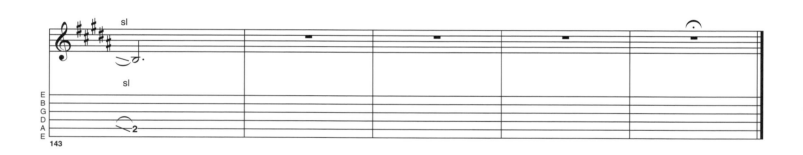

Satch Boogie

Music by
Joe Satriani

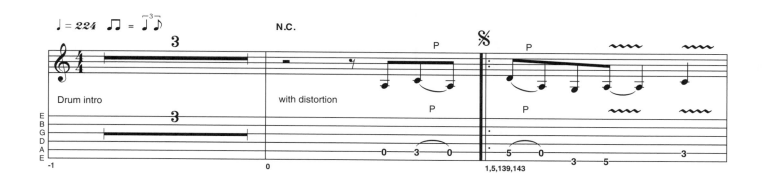

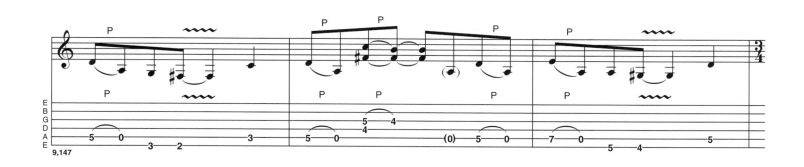

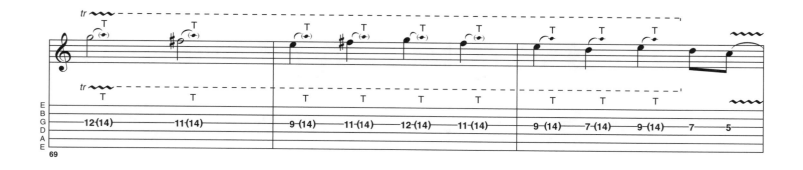

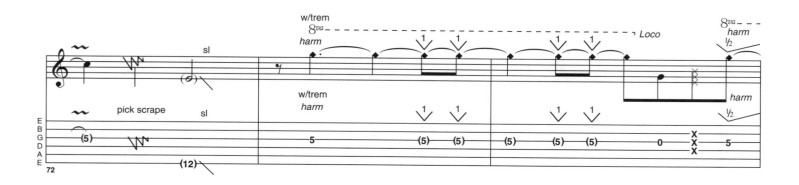

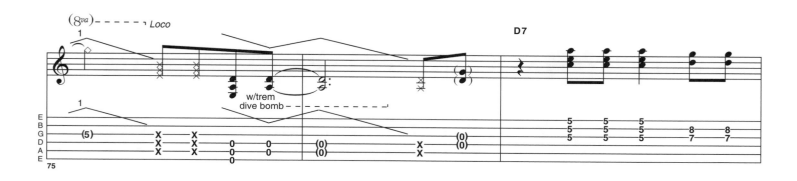

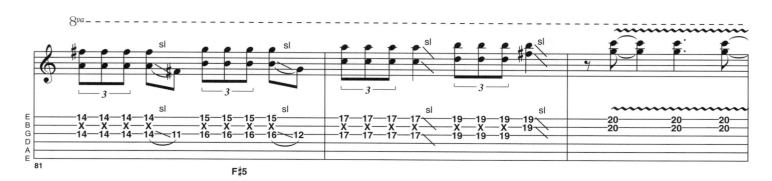

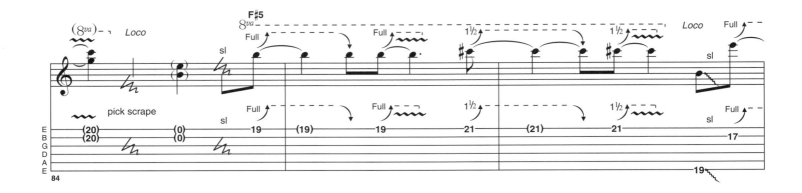

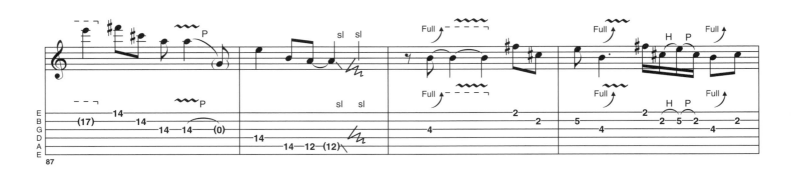

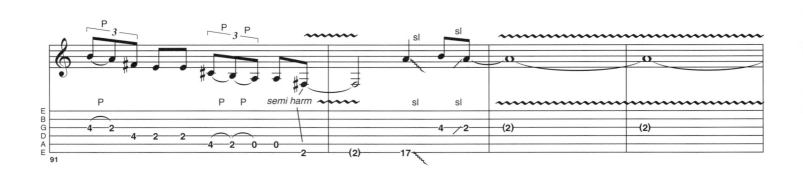

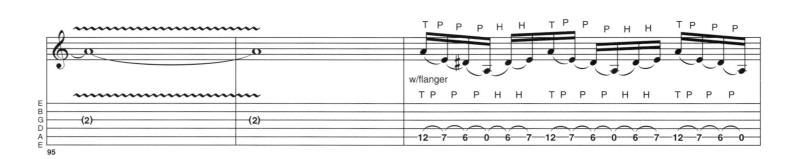

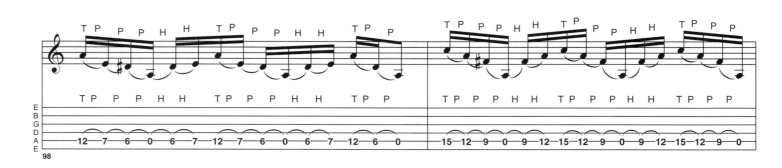

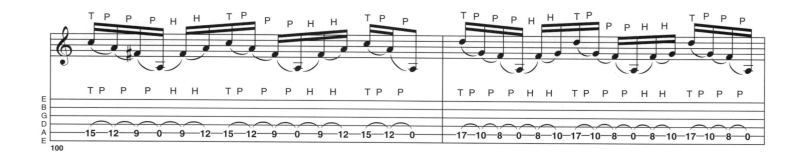

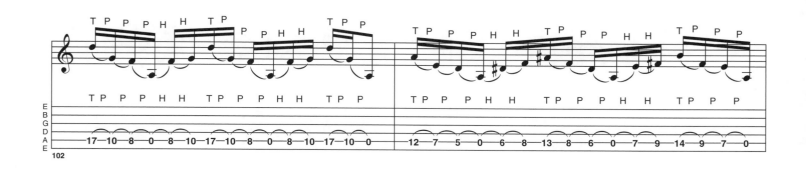

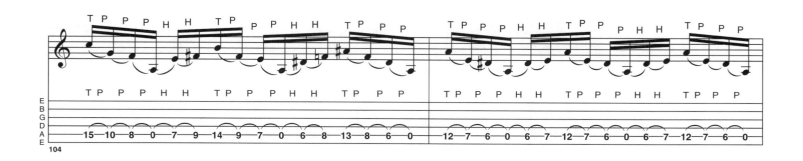

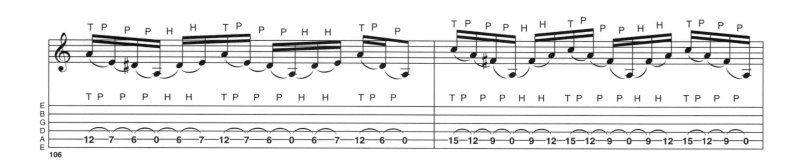

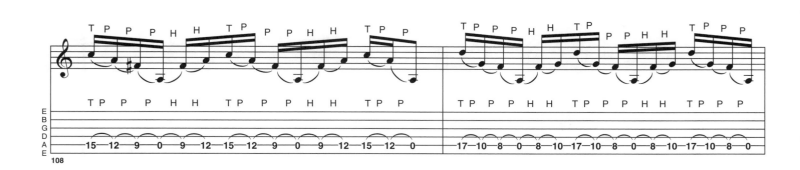

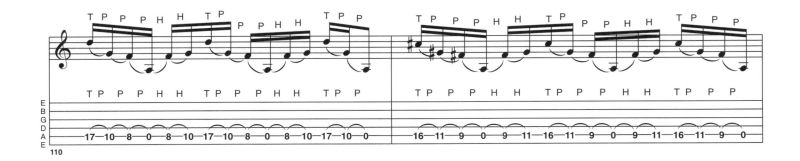

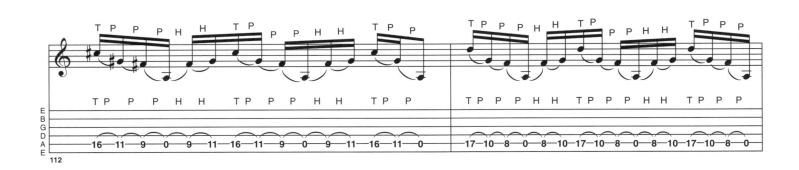

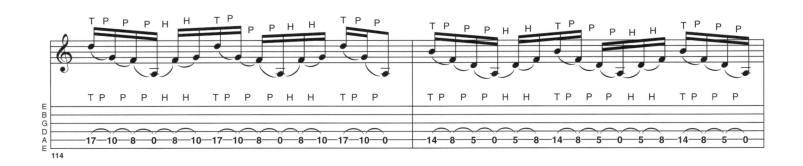

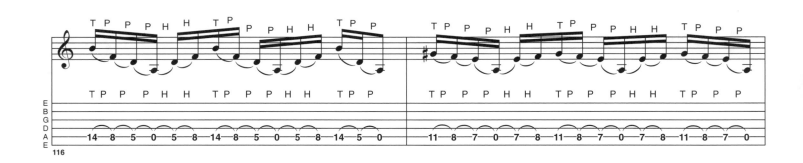

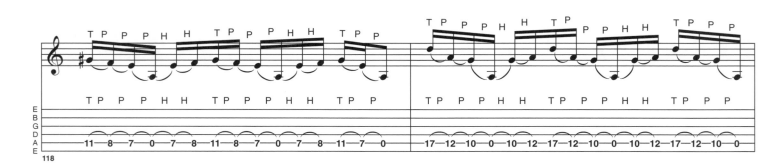

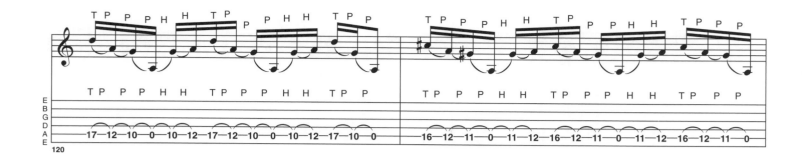

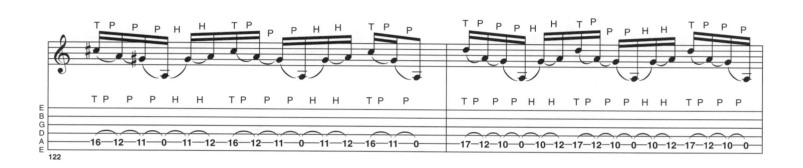

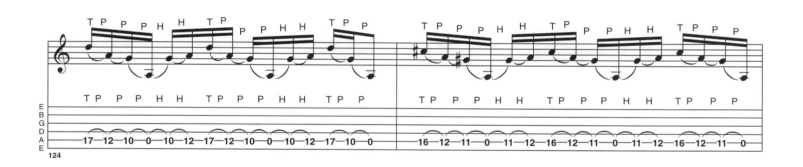

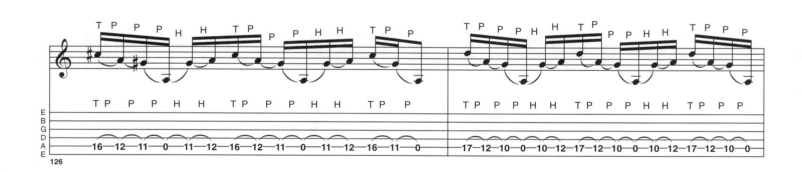

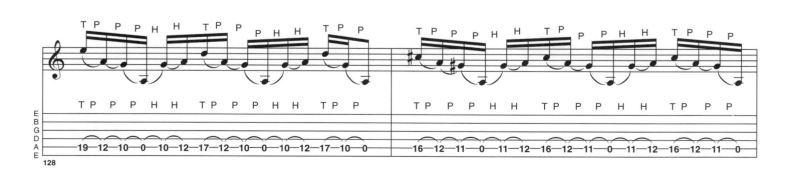

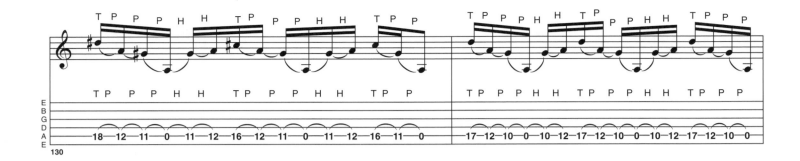

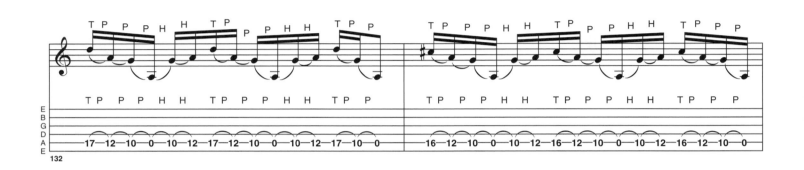

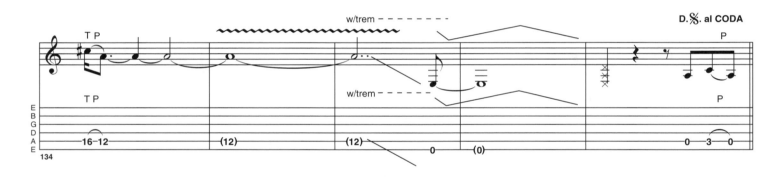

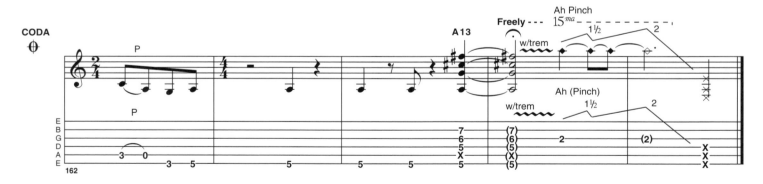

Circles

Music by
Joe Satriani

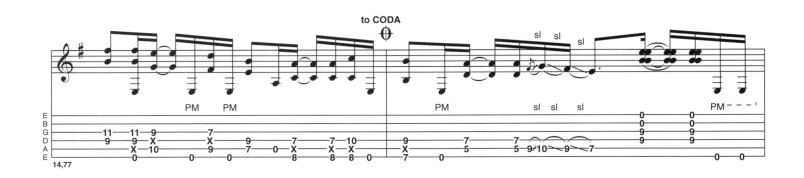

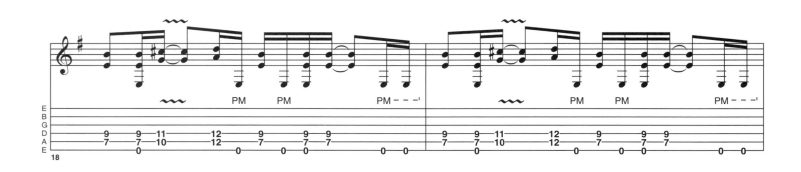

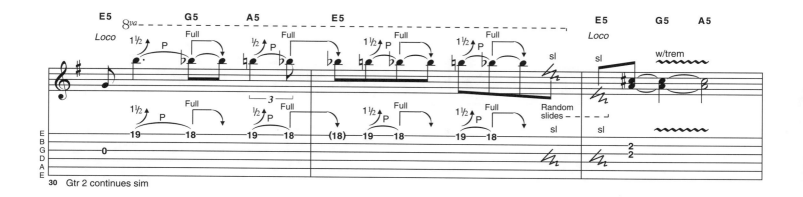

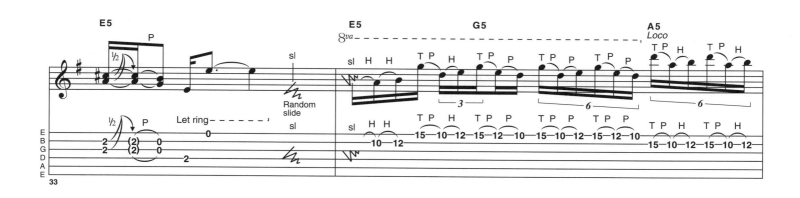

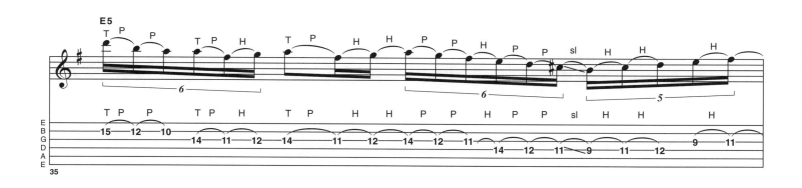

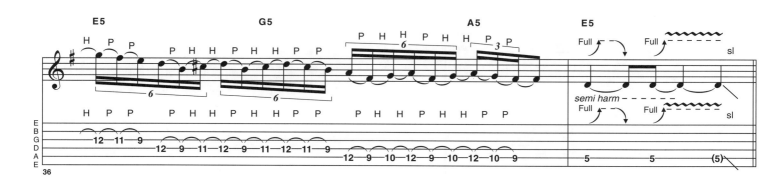

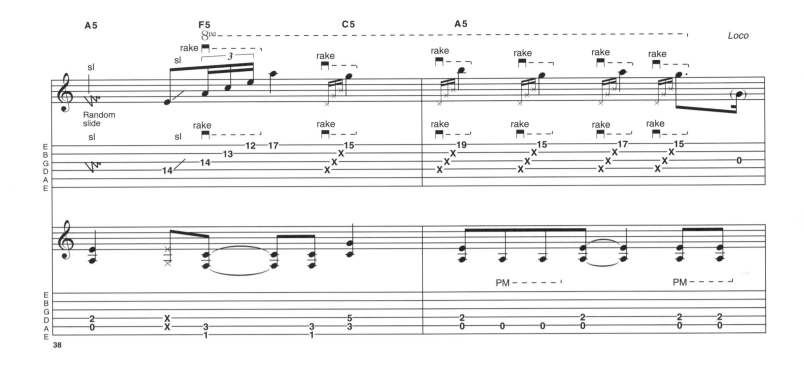

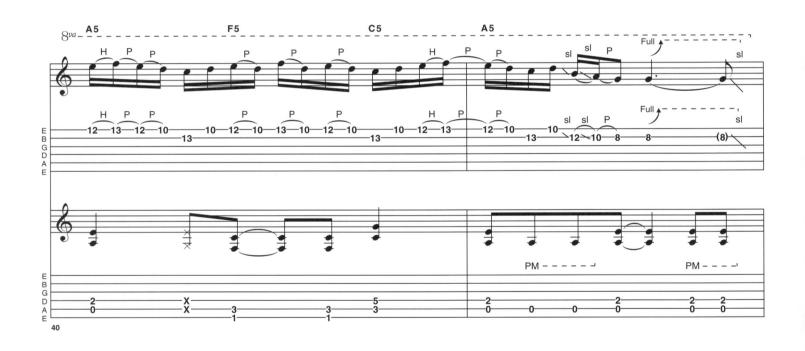

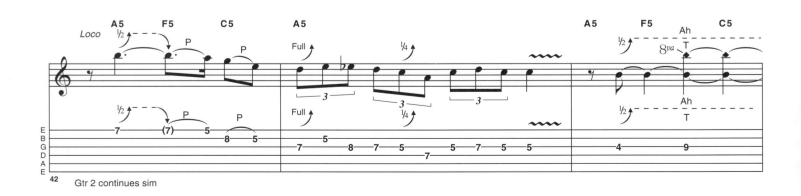

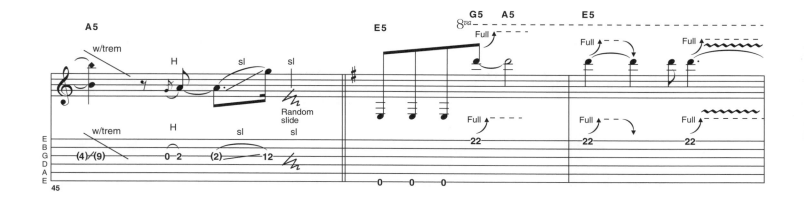

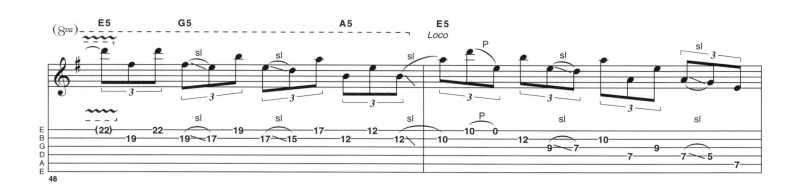

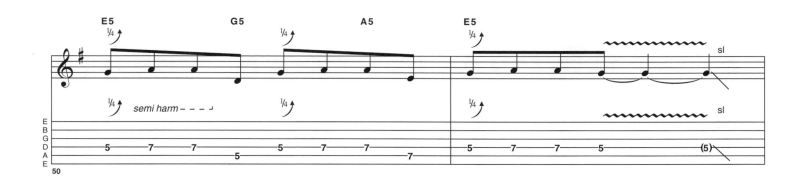

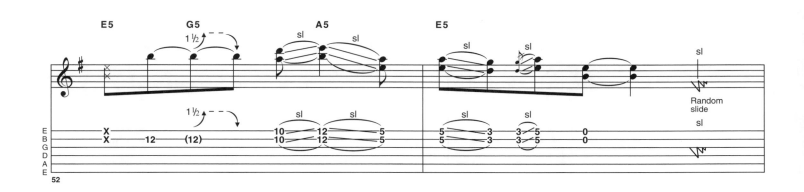

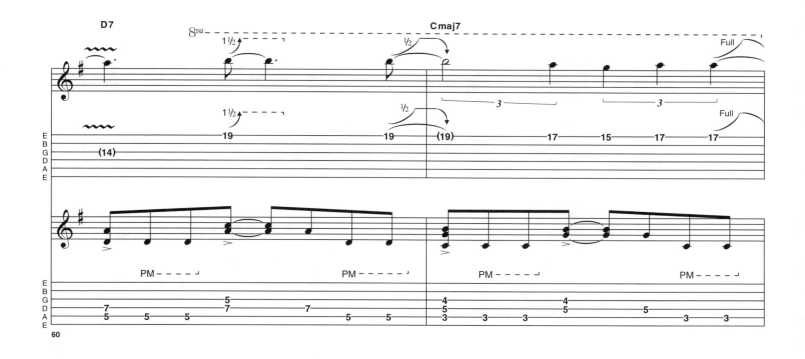

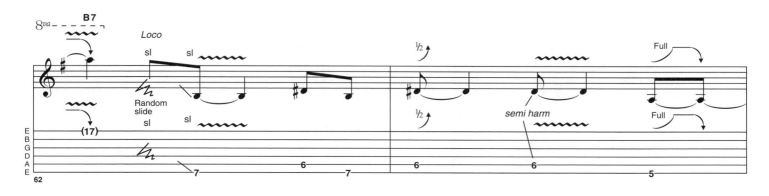

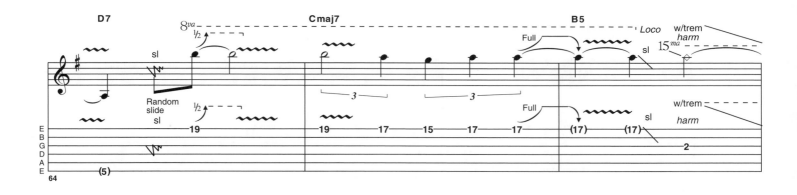

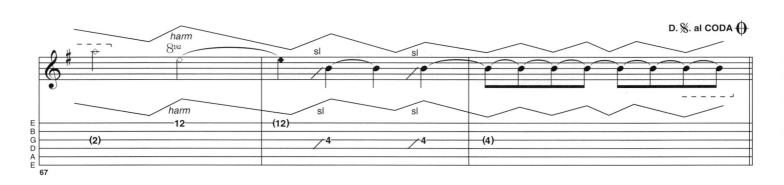

CODA

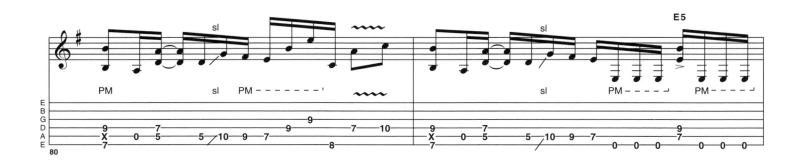

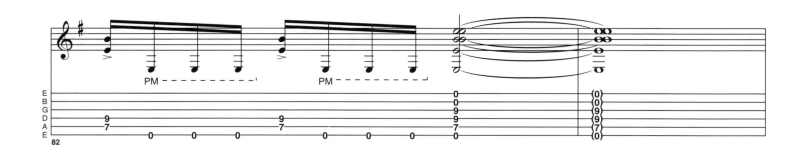

The Extremist

Music by
Joe Satriani

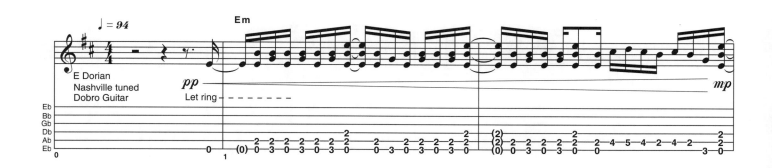

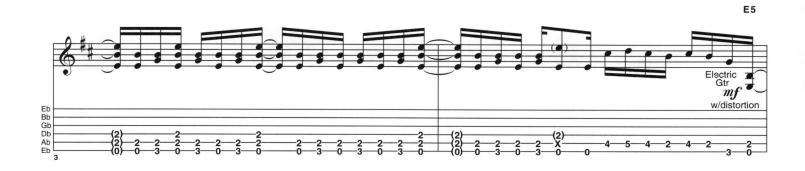

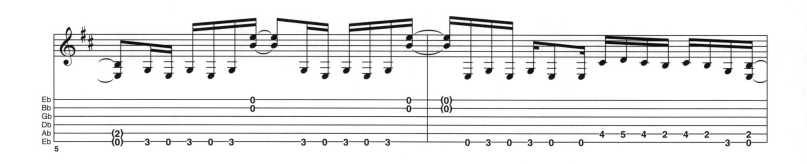

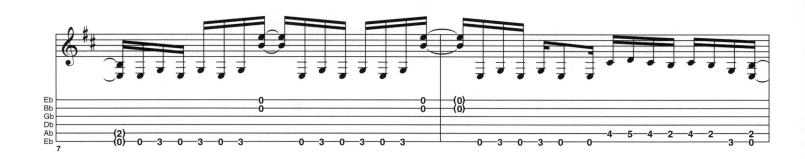

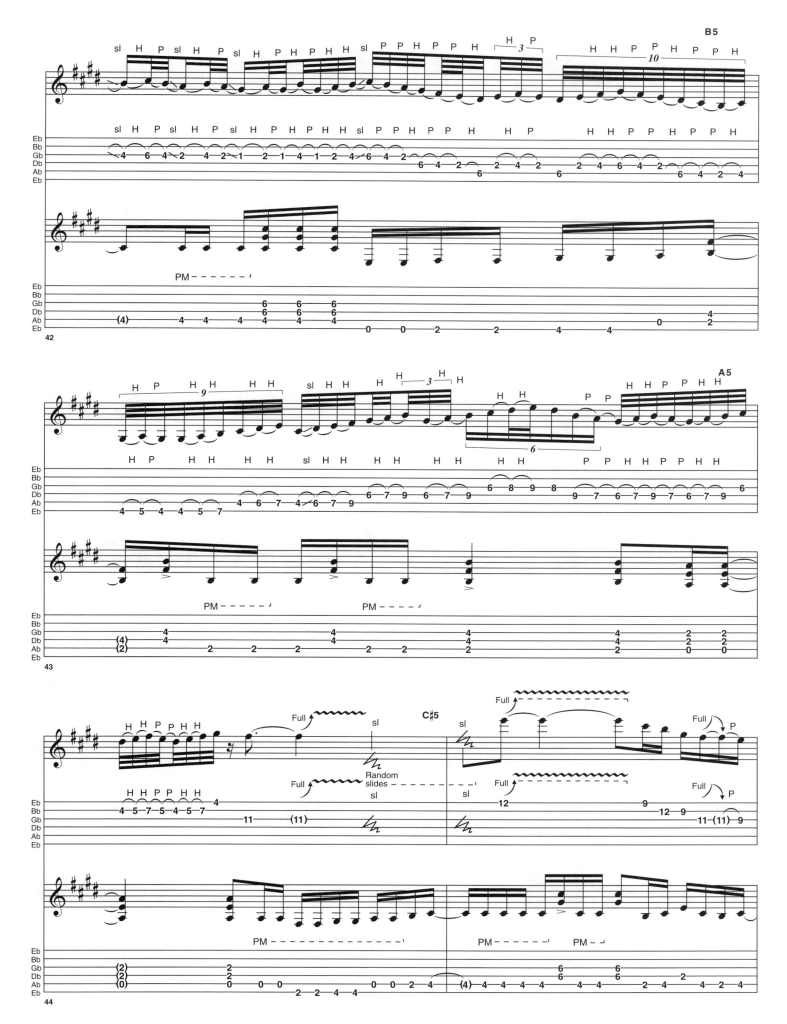

* Operate trem w/LH.
  Depress bar before striking note.

** Random pinched harmonics
   produced over pickups.

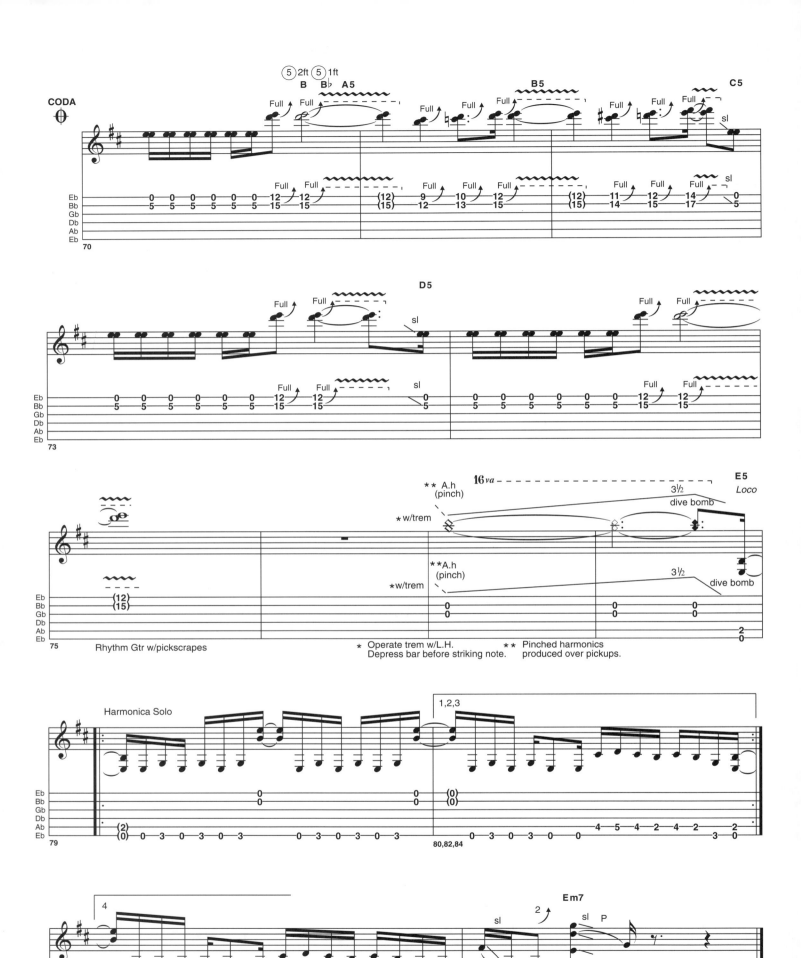

THE HOTTEST TAB SONGBOOKS AVAILABLE FOR GUITAR & BASS!

PLAY IT LIKE IT IS GUITAR
WITH TABLATURE

NOTE-FOR-NOTE TRANSCRIPTIONS

PLAY IT LIKE IT IS BASS
WITH TABLATURE

NOTE-FOR-NOTE TRANSCRIPTIONS

from **CHERRY LANE MUSIC COMPANY**

Quality in Printed Music

Guitar Transcriptions

Bass Transcriptions

FOR MORE INFORMATION, SEE YOUR LOCAL MUSIC DEALER, OR WRITE TO:

HAL•LEONARD® CORPORATION
7777 W. BLUEMOUND RD. P.O. BOX 13819 MILWAUKEE, WI 53213

Prices, contents and availability subject to change without notice.

CHERRY LANE MUSIC COMPANY

6 East 32nd Street, New York, NY 10016

Quality in Printed Music

The Magazine You Can Play

Visit the Guitar One web site at **www.guitarone.com**

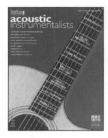

ACOUSTIC INSTRUMENTALISTS
INCLUDES TAB

Over 15 transcriptions from legendary artists such as Leo Kottke, John Fahey, Jorma Kaukonen, Chet Atkins, Adrian Legg, Jeff Beck, and more.

02500399 Play-It-Like-It-Is Guitar............................$9.95

THE BEST BASS LINES
INCLUDES TAB

24 super songs: Bohemian Rhapsody • Celebrity Skin • Crash Into Me • Crazy Train • Glycerine • Money • November Rain • Smoke on the Water • Sweet Child O' Mine • What Would You Say • You're My Flavor • and more.
02500311 Play-It-Like-It-Is Bass $14.95

BLUES TAB
INCLUDES TAB

14 songs: Boom Boom • Cold Shot • Hide Away • I Can't Quit You Baby • I'm Your Hoochie Coochie Man • In 2 Deep • It Hurts Me Too • Talk to Your Daughter • The Thrill Is Gone • and more.
02500410 Play-It-Like-It-Is Guitar............................$14.95

CLASSIC ROCK TAB
INCLUDES TAB

15 rock hits: Cat Scratch Fever • Crazy Train • Day Tripper • Hey Joe • Hot Blooded • Start Me Up • We Will Rock You • You Really Got Me • and more.
02500408 Play-It-Like-It-Is Guitar............................$14.95

MODERN ROCK TAB
INCLUDES TAB

15 of modern rock's best: Are You Gonna Go My Way • Denial • Hanging by a Moment • I Did It • My Hero • Nobody's Real • Rock the Party (Off the Hook) • Shock the Monkey • Slide • Spit It Out • and more.
02500409 Play-It-Like-It-Is Guitar............................$14.95

SIGNATURE SONGS
INCLUDES TAB

21 artists' trademark hits: Crazy Train (Ozzy Osbourne) • My Generation (The Who) • Smooth (Santana) • Sunshine of Your Love (Cream) • Walk This Way (Aerosmith) • Welcome to the Jungle (Guns N' Roses) • What Would You Say (Dave Matthews Band) • and more.
02500303 Play-It-Like-It-Is Guitar............................$16.95

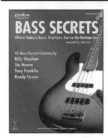

BASS SECRETS
WHERE TODAY'S BASS STYLISTS GET TO THE BOTTOM LINE
compiled by John Stix
Bass Secrets brings together 48 columns highlighting specific topics – ranging from the technical to the philosophical – from masters such as Stu Hamm, Randy Coven, Tony Franklin and Billy Sheehan. They cover topics including tapping, walking bass lines, soloing, hand positions, harmonics and more. Clearly illustrated with musical examples.
02500100 ....$12.95

CLASSICS ILLUSTRATED
WHERE BACH MEETS ROCK
by Robert Phillips
Classics Illustrated is designed to demonstrate for readers and players the links between rock and classical music. Each of the 30 columns from *Guitar* highlights one musical concept and provides clear examples in both styles of music. This cool book lets you study moving bass lines over stationary chords in the music of Bach and Guns N' Roses, learn the similarities between "Leyenda" and "Diary of a Madman," and much more!
02500101 ....$9.95

GUITAR SECRETS
INCLUDES TAB
WHERE ROCK'S GUITAR MASTERS SHARE THEIR TRICKS, TIPS & TECHNIQUES
compiled by John Stix
This unique and informative compilation features 42 columns culled from *Guitar* magazine. Readers will discover dozens of techniques and playing tips, and gain practical advice and words of wisdom from guitar masters.
02500099 ....$10.95

IN THE LISTENING ROOM
WHERE ARTISTS CRITIQUE THE MUSIC OF THEIR PEERS
compiled by John Stix
A compilation of 75 columns from *Guitar* magazine, *In the Listening Room* provides a unique opportunity for readers to hear major recording artists remark on the music of their peers. These artists were given no information about what they would hear, and their comments often tell as much about themselves as they do about the music they listened to. Includes candid critiques by music legends like Aerosmith, Jeff Beck, Jack Bruce, Dimebag Darrell, Buddy Guy, Kirk Hammett, Eric Johnson, John McLaughlin, Dave Navarro, Carlos Santana, Joe Satriani, Stevie Ray Vaughan, and many others.
02500097 ....$14.95

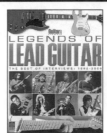

LEGENDS OF LEAD GUITAR
THE BEST OF INTERVIEWS: 1995-2000
This is a fascinating compilation of interviews with today's greatest guitarists! From deeply rooted blues giants to the most fearless pioneers, legendary players reveal how they achieve their extraordinary craft.
02500329 ....$14.95

LESSON LAB

This exceptional book/CD pack features more than 20 in-depth lessons. Tackle in detail a variety of pertinent music- and guitar-related subjects, such as scales, chords, theory, guitar technique, songwriting, and much more!
02500330 Book/CD Pack.......................$19.95

NOISE & FEEDBACK

THE BEST OF 1995-2000: YOUR QUESTIONS ANSWERED
If you ever wanted to know about a specific guitar lick, trick, technique or effect, this book/CD pack is for you! It features over 70 lessons on composing • computer assistance • education and career advice • equipment • technique • terminology and notation • tunings • and more.
02500328 Book/CD Pack.......................$17.95

OPEN EARS
A JOURNEY THROUGH LIFE WITH GUITAR IN HAND
by Steve Morse
In this collection of 50 *Guitar* magazine columns from the mid-'90s on, guitarist Steve Morse sets the story straight about what being a working musician *really* means. He deals out practical advice on: playing with the band, songwriting, recording and equipment, and more, through anecdotes of his hard-knock lessons learned.
02500333 ....$10.95

SPOTLIGHT ON STYLE

THE BEST OF 1995-2000: AN EXPLORER'S GUIDE TO GUITAR
This book and CD cover 18 of the world's most popular guitar styles, including: blues guitar • classical guitar • country guitar • funk guitar • jazz guitar • Latin guitar • metal • rockabilly and more!
02500320 Book/CD Pack.......................$19.95

STUDIO CITY
PROFESSIONAL SESSION RECORDING FOR GUITARISTS
by Carl Verheyen
In this collection of colomns from Guitar Magazine, guitarists will learn how to: exercise studio etiquette and act professionally • acquire, assemble and set up gear for sessions • use the tricks of the trade to become a studio hero • get repeat call-backs • and more.
02500195 ....$9.95